KU-605-584

South Dublin Libraries

www.southdublinlibraries.ie

'*Out of the Woods* had me hooked. Refreshing, frank, edifying, courageous . . . I was quite emotional by the end. Luke Turner is a serious thinker and a unique and important new voice'

Amy Liptrot, author of *The Outrun*

'Unflinching on relationships, the nature of obsession, lust, masculinity, faith and lost innocence. *Out of the Woods* is a very special book' Brett Anderson

'A transformative, brutally honest memoir which is un-afraid to stalk the monster that hides in the darkest of forests . . . one of my books of the year' John Higgs

'A brave and beautiful book, electrifying on sex and nature, religion and love. No one is writing quite like this'

Olivia Laing

'A powerful testament to the redemptive power of – loving, determinedly – making what was hidden known'

Helen Jukes, author of *A Honeybee Heart Has Five Openings*

'Emotionally and sexually charged, deeply moving, with hauntingly exquisite writing and an extraordinary command of language . . . Such raw honesty is precious and makes for a powerful read' Cosey Fanni Tutti

'Like nothing I've read before, rich, honest, humane and thoughtful, it is utterly original and really gets into the bones' Lucy Jones

South Dublin Libraries www.south...

'This is a book to get lost in . . . A disturbing trauma narrative, it's also a work of delightfully low, pants-dropping comedy, and a learned meditation'

Sukhdev Sandhu, *Guardian*

'Turns the nature memoir genre upon its head . . . *Out of the Woods* is a book full of poetry and pathos. More than anything it is a bold and beautiful study of how to be a true modern man'　　　　　　　Ben Myers, *Spectator*

'Achieves that tricky balance of feeling both deeply personal and totally universal'　　　　　　　　　*Esquire*

'Truly beautiful prose . . . the candour and insightful scholarship Turner brings to his subject make it a very worthwhile read'　　　　Grub Smith, *Literary Review*

'Honest, haunting and moving, *Out of the Woods* envelops you in its leafy, sprawling pages, and squeezes tight. Captivating and poignant'　　　　　　　　*Attitude*

'Turner mixes vulnerability with the sort of insight that comes only through a complex honesty'

Sean Hewitt, *Irish Times*

Luke Turner is a writer, editor and curator based in London. He co-founded and edits the influential online music publication *The Quietus* and regularly writes on music, culture and place for a variety of magazines, websites and broadcasters. *Out of the Woods* is his first book.

OUT OF THE WOODS

Luke Turner

WEIDENFELD & NICOLSON

First published in Great Britain in 2019 by Weidenfeld & Nicolson
This paperback edition published in 2020 by Weidenfeld & Nicolson
an imprint of The Orion Publishing Group Ltd
Carmelite House, 50 Victoria Embankment
London EC4Y 0DZ

An Hachette UK Company

1 3 5 7 9 10 8 6 4 2

Copyright © Luke Turner 2019

The moral right of Luke Turner to be identified as
the author of this work has been asserted in accordance
with the Copyright, Designs and Patents Act of 1988.

All rights reserved. No part of this publication may be
reproduced, stored in a retrieval system, or transmitted in any
form or by any means, electronic, mechanical, photocopying,
recording, or otherwise, without the prior permission of both
the copyright owner and the above publisher of this book.

A CIP catalogue record for this book is
available from the British Library.

ISBN (Mass Market Paperback) 978 1 4746 0716 2
ISBN (eBook) 978 1 4746 0717 9

Typeset by Input Data Services Ltd, Somerset

Printed and bound in Great Britain by Clays Ltd, Elcograf S.p.A.

MIX
Paper from
responsible sources
FSC® C104740

www.orionbooks.co.uk
www.weidenfeldandnicolson.co.uk

To Mum and Dad,
for your love, grace and understanding

Contents

Midway upon the journey of our life
I found myself within a forest dark,
For the straightforward pathway had been lost.

Ah me! how hard a thing it is to say
What was this forest savage, rough, and stern,
Which in the very thought renews the fear.

So bitter is it, death is little more;
But of the good to treat, which there I found,
Speak will I of the other things I saw there.

Dante, *The Inferno*, Canto I

I

The Man in the Forest

As a child I entered Epping Forest through a picture. The Victorian print on the magnolia wall of my parents' living room was the portal that took me there. Branches reached out from the black and white ink into a dismal glade, threatening to drag me into their hollow, secret places, their gnarls and whorls. In the sky, wind-blown scraps of birds. A man, ragged and set about in the gale, trudging slowly towards the dark mass of the distant forest. He seemed so insubstantial to me, an inhuman wraith or perhaps a man doomed, about to be swallowed up and never released. I knelt on a chair and stared at this picture for hours, at once compelled by it yet struck by an unnerving dread.

Now, at the age of thirty-six, I found myself sitting opposite a man just like the etched wanderer in the kitchen of my uncle and aunty's house in Theydon Bois, a village towards the northern end of the forest. I won't refer to him by name because he doesn't want to be found. I don't want to take away his Epping Forest, a

1

place he couldn't have expected to see again on that day a few years ago when he climbed onto a chair, fastened a dog leash to a light fitting and fashioned a noose to put round his neck.

The man who lived in the forest was matter-of-fact and bright-eyed that morning. My aunty passed him a biscuit and asked what had happened to the mobile phone he'd been given in case of emergencies, when he was alone in his camp somewhere out in the woods. He looked at her, bemused. 'I don't mind,' he said. 'I'm a forest spirit. I'm just more content getting rid of the radio, the telephone, the trappings.'

It was a dreary day in the middle of a mild January, and across the road the trunks of Epping Forest were an unforgiving grey, dormant now until spring, lifeless as sculptures made of steel slag. Outside the kitchen door, chaffinches and coal tits negotiated their shifts on a container stuffed with pumpkin seeds. My eyes were drawn to a ghostly outline on the window where the attack of a sparrowhawk – not spotting the panes of glass that separated it from the trees of Epping Forest – on a feeding songbird had thumped to a premature conclusion, its near-death captured with an imprint of oily wings.

The man was almost seventy, stood around six feet tall and held himself solidly, despite an awkward gait caused by severe arthritis. His head was bald on top, but hair, yellow-white nicotine curtains, curled down his neck into a gloriously unkempt beard that was frayed at the edges, like half-hearted winter ice on a pond. His skin was deeply grooved and tanned a rich brown that seemed at odds with a life spent under the trees. Beneath fox-whisker brows his large, round eyes were an intense blue. He peered at me inquisitively, clearly wondering who I was and why I was there. The week before, my aunty had intercepted him on his morning walk to the Costa coffee machine in Tesco to ask if he wouldn't mind stopping by. To be honest, I was as perplexed as he was. I was distracted, conscious that the last time I'd been in this house everything had been different.

Over the decade and a half I'd lived in London, rising rents had forced me to make my way from the centre out towards Epping Forest, from the edges of the city in Old Street to Hackney and eventually Walthamstow. I'd moved there a few years before with my girlfriend, Alice, and when I entered through the front door for the first time my impulse had been to race upstairs and look out of the bedroom window. Over the William Morris Gallery and beyond the streets of the suburb of Chingford I could see past London, where Epping Forest was a green slab against the late-summer haze. I imagined everything beneath that rich canopy was peaceful and green. The warm smell of beech leaves. The birdsong and the filtered light. I had dreamed of living near this landscape for years.

During a childhood moving around the country, Epping Forest was the one constant. Both my parents had grown up on the edge of the forest, and I loved Dad's stories about school break-times when he'd be allowed to run across the road and play amid the trees. My mum remembered how her brothers would go into the forest at night to watch badgers, and build dams across the streams. It had ignited in Mum and Dad a love of the natural world that was intricately bound up with their Christian faith. It had seemed idyllic to imagine this semi-wilderness on the doorstep rather than the football games and dog walkers of the dull municipal park we lived near in a town a half-hour drive east along the M25. I'd spend hours drawing imaginary maps of the forest's Lost Pond. When we'd visit my uncle, he'd take me for walks and teach me the names of trees and how to identify them by their bark and foliage, and we'd balance huge branches on our shoulders to take home for his fire.

Years later, living with the forest hovering at the edge of my field of vision turned my casual interest into an obsession. Every morning and evening, as I stood cleaning my teeth, dribbling toothpaste over the carpet and piled-up clean washing, I would stare out towards the horizon where, on a clear day, the spire of High Beach Church could be seen, a pinprick above the trees against the sky. As a kid I could access the forest on a family visit or via that transporting picture on the wall. Now it was mine, whenever I might want it. It was always changing, this distant view beyond the rooftops of the suburbs. In the spring and summer it was a slowly evolving smear of greens. In the autumn the dirty browns and oranges were tempered by rain and mist. Winter treetops made a steely line against the glow from the lights of the Metropolitan Police's helicopter base on the far side of the forest at Lippitt's Hill. Once, as I was returning home at 3 a.m. after a midweek rave, a huge electrical storm encircled

London. I stood naked at the door, watching the forest explode like a blown-out negative as Alice tried to sleep behind me.

If I left our front door, turned right and then right again past the William Morris Gallery, then walked for ten minutes along Forest Road via the recently gentrified Bell pub, a sex shop that probably gave its last thrill around the turn of the millennium, two chip shops and a Homebase, I would come to Waterworks Roundabout, where cattle grids buzz incongruously under the wheels of cars heading onto the North Circular. From here you can dive into the forest, and be under the cover of its leaves before emerging into the open fields of Essex – a twelve-mile-long, 6,000-acre green snake of beech, hornbeam, common oak and silver birch from the edges of the urban and suburban, from London's East End to the Essex countryside beyond.

My first year living with this view was a time of stability and happiness. For a while I felt as if some of the struggles that had shaped my first three decades might have been banished by this sensible domesticity within sight of the forest. In simple rituals I would try and imbue every aspect of my life with its presence. Alice and I would take carrier bags to bring back wood from the forest for our open fire just as my parents had to theirs, and I'd sit and watch the flames take, feeling a rare contentment. The smoke from our chimney was a signal back to the forest that I had finally come home. I experienced it as a place of quiet reflection and contemplation, as millions of happy souls do their favourite landscapes.

It was not to last; for my family Epping Forest has always been a place of both beginnings and endings.

That morning, before I'd driven a borrowed car to visit the man who lived in the forest, I'd awoken on a narrow foam mattress in the dusty box room of my friends' house. I'd been there a few months, a more-than-temporary place to crash after I'd had to leave the home I shared with Alice when our relationship slowly crumbled away a few months before. It hardly felt like any time at all since we'd been in bed knackered after days trying to clear the mass of builder's rubble and bramble from the bombsite back garden, texting about dinner, or inadvertently spending a night sharing a bottle of gin during those lubricated, intimate conversations that can hold a relationship together. One evening we took the train to Chingford and strolled towards Yates' Meadow and my favourite view over London. When the sun dipped and sent the treetops on the opposite slope into cobbled relief, the light might have affirmed that we were on the right journey, together. I felt a gnawing when it didn't.

There had been no explosion, no betrayal. When any relationship ends we fail to pinpoint the exact moment at which the worry that something is amiss becomes its own logic, a potent, destructive and irresistible force. Much of it was my fault. Once again, my sexual orientation had begun to flow in confused directions and I struggled against the binary rules of heteronormative love. At the same time, long-standing, hardwired compulsions had started to make their presence known,

6

demanding to be answered. As I did my best to wrestle with them, I had closed off from her. Upset, she'd reacted by moving out to her sister's place for a week.

I'd spent those days on my own in the house expecting the crisis to blow over. I took a group of pals for a Sunday walk in the forest and tried to put a brave face on it all, unwilling to accept the path that was emerging in my life. A couple on the walk had recently split up. It was awkward, but they seemed fine. It set to work a tiny niggle in the back of my mind that I, or those old compulsions, might want my relationship to go a similar way. Yet when later that evening Alice came back to the house and said she knew it was over, I collapsed to the floor of the bedroom that looked out towards Epping Forest, face scraping the rough carpet, and screamed. When she asked me to move out a few days later, I couldn't bear to take a final look at the view.

Back on that January morning, the dregs of my tea had turned as cold as the misty forest outside. My thoughts wandered to the sickness in the belly that is a symptom of a future wrenched away. I desperately wished that I could draw some comfort from the words of the man who lived in the forest as he told me how he'd decided not to die that day under his makeshift noose, but had come to live in his tent on the other side of Genesis Slade instead. 'I was trying to be happy,' he said. 'If I get myself into a bad position, I will very strongly think, "I like this." Mind over matter, cause and effect.'

I stayed for a while longer. My uncle and aunty wanted to know what had happened with Alice, of whom they'd been very fond. I tried to put a positive spin on it, though I wasn't feeling it at all. As soon as I had to speak of her a voice inside my head would strike up a counter-narrative against the words coming out of my mouth. It wasn't the right thing to do, that quiet interior murmur told me. I still loved her. And deeper and more secretly still, the rush as soon as we'd broken up to feel the naked press of a man on top of me had only made me feel more confused. It was the latest manifestation of a self-destructive pattern that had disrupted my life since my teenage years. I watched the logs from Epping Forest catch in the grate of the fire that as a kid I'd loved to stoke, and felt myself sink into regret.

That morning I'd parked the borrowed car badly, somehow managing to impale it on a branch, and it took ages of metal screeching on wood to untangle. Driving up the hill away from the village into the forest, I caught sight of the man trudging slowly along. I slowed down and tooted the horn and he waved, beard splitting into a grin. I didn't want to go back to the city, but he'd be off for hours now, wandering until dark, talking to his friends be they human, canine, fox or tree. 'I walk and walk and walk, even with my knees,' he'd told me over tea. 'I've got all the time in the world. To see all those things!'

I kept an eye on the rear-view mirror and watched his loping form gradually become indistinct against the violent contortions of the forest behind, my eyes lost thirty years, and there I was, kneeling on an old chair in my parents' living room, the light of evening catching the slow dances of dust and fluff, staring into that picture. That twisted form, lost and buffeted by the weather and nature and endless power of Epping Forest, wasn't the man on the road at all. It was me.

2

The Blizzard of the World

I spent the New Year's Eve after Alice and I broke up with friends in a bungalow down on the north Kent shore of the Thames Estuary. Hungover, and then topping it back up again for the first three days of the new year, I felt an invisible, thick barrier begin to ooze round me as if I had rolled and caked myself in the mud of the river's shallows. I tried to be swept along by the communal jollity of the season in those days but ended up wandering off on my own, for nothing could replace what I had lost.

On New Year's Day I climbed onto a rickety pile of rotting hay bales to try and force the sea air to wash my nausea away and looked upriver, towards London. I wondered who Alice might have kissed at midnight. New Years we'd shared before came flooding back – by a river in Devon, laughing at the pensioners dancing on a table as if it were a boat on the beer-soaked sea of the pub floor, or the night she'd tried to cut my hair with the kitchen scissors and left me with hacked tramlines before we went out to lose ourselves in each other at a never-ending rave.

A familiar voice started muttering in the back of my head and, without thinking, I switched on Grindr. A hopeful man with a St George's cross profile picture over on the north bank in Southend offered to get in his van and drive across the QEII Bridge to fuck me. He was persistent. I deleted the app, again. There's nothing like the offer of a pounding from a plumber to make you feel utterly alone.

I had hoped that the New Year trip would be a fresh start, that the natural ebb of life would soon smooth the jagged promontories of loss and my painful memories. I had forgotten that it takes many tides to wash the dirt of London down the Thames and out into the North Sea, and for months it had felt impossible to make headway against the flow.

The lust of London is so time- and energy-sapping that those who have been consumed by it often find it hard to leave, even for a moment. In the decade or so before I'd moved nearer to the forest and it'd become part of my life again, I'd only rarely ventured up there. Back then, it was a place of memory shaped by child-hood fancy. When Alice and I broke up and I had to leave the house that looked over the distant forest, I started to feel my connection with that place fracture. The two relationships had become so entwined with my adult identity that when one clunked off track it disrupted everything else. I wanted the forest back, to reclaim it as I saw it as a child, as if those maps I'd drawn might come alive around me and give me shelter against the sickening loss I was struggling to face.

Again and again during that damp and mildewed winter I travelled up to Chingford and Loughton to trudge around the oozing woodland. I borrowed Dad's Epping Forest history books to absorb the place in every way I could. A friend told me the London Metropolitan Archives were free to access and I spent hours leafing through crumbling Victorian documents – keepers' reports, formal orders for hams, uniforms and adzes, ammo for squirrel hunts, newspaper cuttings about conservation campaigns and murders. When faced with the deathly silent grief of the end of love, my instinct was to obscure it with a hurricane of distraction, day and night, from forest and London alike. I whirled from that thin foam mattress to work, snatched hours in the archives or up in the forest before heavy pub sessions or another Tinder or Grindr date. On too many mornings the unfamiliar light of an unknown bedroom and a stranger's warmth next to me would stab through the hangover with a panicking awareness of all I had lost.

One evening, after a walk that had yet again failed to clear my mind, I read a news story about a tribe deep in the Brazilian jungle that had recently been photographed from the air for the first time. If it was that Epping Forest print on my parents' wall that had haunted my impressionable younger years, it was this digital image, screen-grabbed and saved onto my phone, that consumed me now. I still have it. The rich green of the canopy broken by a pustule, a clearing in which a circular structure had been built. A gap of a few metres between the rich growth of the surrounding trees and seventeen large rectangular mats of dried thatch that touched the ground on the forest side, each rising to sit atop a strut to form a simple hut. It was a maloca, an encampment of a sub-group the Yanomami people called the Moxihatetema. Shielded against the murk of the trees beyond, in those mats of leaves and vines under which fires would burn at night we see reflected an ancient human desire to separate ourselves from the forest. Nothing has changed, save for the materials with which we build our huts. What were once tiny settlements like the Moxihatetema's maloca would eventually become London and all the other cities of the world that displaced the forests and filled up with people who feared them.

It's only in recent years that the commonly held view that Britain and Northern Europe have always been covered in an impenetrable mass of continuous forest was revised, and a far more complex picture emerged. If in 2006 even the late, great arboreal expert Oliver Rackham wrote in the last edition of his seminal book *Woodlands* that he had previously been mistaken about the matter, then we may also now question how that myth of an untouched, primeval forest which we humans invaded might have shaped our understanding of ourselves. One afternoon, trying to distract myself from yet another fruitless search to find somewhere permanent to live, I discovered that recent research into genetic distribution at the end of the last Ice Age reveals that humans hadn't retreated south into the woods with the glaciers' advance, but instead lived predominantly in tree-scattered savanna, the predecessor of the open woodland pasture that once characterised the Epping Forest landscape. Here the trees were more easily cut and manipulated than within the forest, providing not just fire for warmth and cooking but shelter, refuge from predators and weapons with which to hunt the larger game that roamed the more open land. I wondered what they would have made of the dense woodland beyond the plains.

As the ice sheets melted 10,000 years ago, *Homo sapiens* and trees alike began to move north, mounting a parallel invasion of what was once lost under ice. Maps charting the return of trees to Britain show, species by species, their lines of advance across the land: oak occupying Cornwall by 9500 BC, and a mere 500 years later reaching a band stretching from north Norfolk across the English Midlands to Snowdonia and the Llyn Peninsula. I thought of the humans who might already have inhabited that landscape: before the melting ice filled the English Channel and North Sea, Britain was still connected to the European continental mass and people can surely colonise a land mass far more quickly than trees. Just look at a map showing the return of trees to the British Isles, arrows indicating the direction of invasion – oak from the south-west, pines from the south-east and birch from the east – and you see an arboreal take on the advancing Nazi arrows in the opening credits of *Dad's Army*.

If our Ice Age ancestors had kept away from the dense forests in their warmer, more open refugia far to the south, and some of their immediate descendants saw the trees advancing towards them like Birnham Wood fulfilling the witches' prophecy in *Macbeth*, it's no wonder we have a complex and uneasy relationship with our woodlands. Anyone who has sat around a campfire in a wooded area knows how the dancing fingers of the flames make the surrounding trees start to move, flickering against an impossible blackness beyond. With fire we lost our night vision, and forests became menacing places where predators or foes beyond material comprehension might lurk.

This potential to flip from the rational to terror is especially pronounced when the forest butts up hard against the very edge of a settlement. Like the trees looming behind the cowering roofs of the huts of the Moxihatetema camp, Epping Forest lurks at the end of otherwise unremarkable suburban streets, where on winter evenings it gives the eerie appearance of a civilisation ending in a black void under a fringe of twigs. Epping Forest might not be the largest in Britain, but no other forest adjoins London, that dizzying, truculent, maddening, ambiguous and chaotic beast that impacts on a forest as well as it might a life or a mind.

Perhaps it isn't surprising that I couldn't escape the city and a life that felt broken when I took those short trips out into the ancient woodland, no matter how deep into it I wandered. The city was always there, both surrounding the forest and living inside me. It started to feel uncanny how the two places kept connecting. On Tinder I met a woman whose local surname was familiar to me from many of the old forest documents I had found. I was reeling after a stilted text conversation with Alice in which, however desperate I was to tell her I was still in love with her, the words wouldn't come.

In the pub after work my date told me she lived up in Forest Gate and had just left her partner and kid. Charged with the urgency of two people who, without fuss, know exactly what is needed to temporarily relieve pain, the night gained its own momentum. An hour after meeting we were in a hotel bed; not long after that we decided to go for cocktails in the bar a few floors below. I dressed quickly, but she walked giggling to the lifts naked aside from her coat and boots. As we queued for espresso martinis at the crowded bar she took my hand, pushed it between her legs and whispered, 'Make me come.' Later, when the booze had worn off but we couldn't sleep, I wanted to talk to her about the forest. She wasn't interested. It was just a place where she went for a run.

Yet for me the forest was becoming a place of vulgar chaos, more and more like that dramatic picture that had been on my parents' living-room wall. In half-light the misshapen forms of the trees within the forest seemed to be moving, boiling up out of the ground like lava. The trees of Epping Forest have a fantastical appearance thanks to centuries of pollarding, the process of forest management whereby trees are cut on a regular cycle for firewood or building materials. Once cut, the tree sends up new growth from an increasingly distorted trunk, or bole. Pollarding prolongs a tree's life, but the continuous cutting makes them take on grotesque forms – cows' udders, a pair of buttocks climbing into a hollow, old men's balls, a phallus between thighs, great, heavy, warty growths, welts like parted vulva. I stumbled on one that was the spitting image of Bart's bottle-sucking baby sister Maggie from *The Simpsons*.

Alone as I was in the heart of the darkening wood, the deformed shapes added to my disconcerting awareness that I was surrounded by thousands of living beings, connected by the invisible network of mycelium fungi through which they communicate, send warnings and share nutrients. I felt as if the forest ought to hum, to be whispering around me, to sound alive. But I'd stare at the trees up close and become lost in the whole magical, gigantic organism, silent aside from the sigh of the wind through a billion bare winter twigs. Mute to the human ear it might be, but as my walks increased in frequency my internal conversation with the place ebbed and flowed from a whisper in a silent glade to a rage in the heart of a storm.

In Epping Forest, in any forest, a magic happens that can take us back to our ancient roots. The city is our human superego rendered in bricks and mortar, concrete and glass. In the forest the id cavorts under the pollards. This anxious duality between the civilisation of the city and the forest as a place of licentious abandon and barbarism is one that preoccupies so many of our Western founding myths, religions, philosophy and art. Forests were places where the lust of men might bring about their own destruction. Take the story of Actaeon, a Greek hunter who saw the goddess Artemis bathing naked in a pool. He was overcome by her beauty, but she caught him watching and punished the hapless man by turning him into a stag. Actaeon fled deeper into the forest, but, no longer recognising their master, his own hounds pursued him, wore him down in the chase and tore him apart.

In 1725 the Italian philosopher Giambattista Vico united the cross-cultural neuroses about forests in *The New Science*, one of the most radical texts of the Enlightenment. 'This was the order of human things: first the forests, after that the huts, thence the villages, next the cities and finally the academies', Vico writes. He argues that human history is both cyclical and universal, the evolution from divine, bestial and human occurring over and over again in all the civilisations of the earth, from the Peruvian Indians to German tribes, Cavaliers of Spain, West Indian nobles and the ancient Greeks. It began, according to Vico, with the sons of Noah who after the flood 'descended to a state truly bestial and savage'. The feral children of these people disappeared into the great forest, exerting themselves so hard in trying to penetrate its thick undergrowth that they absorbed nutrients that turned them into giants. They lived without 'that fear of gods, fathers and teachers which chills and benumbs even the most exuberant in childhood'. Eventually, in the sky they saw lightning and imagined that this god was, through the thunder, trying to speak to them. Thus the birth of human imagination, our ability to conceive of something outside ourselves, occurred through the clearings of the forest. As we moved through our bestial state to become learned humans, we developed marriage, religion and burial rituals, cities and education – all, Vico argues, derived from our separation from the forest. If his philosophy is indeed universal, we might, I realised when I first ploughed through *The New Science* that twisted winter, also apply it to ourselves as individuals. Just as Vico saw the human relationship with the forest as being in a state of flux, so we can see ourselves as the same within it, tiny, fleshy blobs of civilisation pushing our way through the trees, flitting between the bestial and the poetic, the sacred and the profane.

It was a duality that I had spent my life struggling to come to terms with. When I was growing up I saw Epping Forest through a child's eyes. It was a simple place of nature that, I had been taught, God created and gave to us. Mum and I would go into the garden with a notebook and together we would draw flowers and weeds, she helping me to write the names of the plants underneath my crude sketches. Later she'd encourage my attempts at gardening, which would result in a few knobbled carrots pulled from the soil and sold on for dinner at 2p apiece. All this was the wonder of creation that she and Dad had thanked Jesus for when saying grace at tea or during night-time prayers. It had all seemed so certain, so pristine.

But Epping Forest has long snared and punctured human dreams and desires, just as its trees are festooned with the glittering remnants of London's helium balloons, released at parties in Bethnal Green and Bow, Clapton and Tottenham, carried by the prevailing south-westerlies only to lose their lift and come to rest on the high ground of the forest. As I was discovering through my obsessive reading of forest histories and rampages through the archives, the cover afforded by its trees and undergrowth will hide a multitude of lurid activities. The sister of a Hell's Angel had told me of a chapter who'd find abusers of children and take them to Epping Forest, strip and bury them up to their necks in soil just loose enough to enable them to escape, before carving the word 'Nonce' into their foreheads and abandoning them. The roads through Epping Forest were historically some of the most dangerous near London, and many of Dick Turpin's most heinous crimes were committed there. The forest's history is stalked by the ghosts of the murdered, suicides and dead babies dumped. But it has also enticed thousands who have found it a place where a true inner self can be discreetly unleashed. I knew there were places, remote car parks and secluded thickets, where men who, like me, had struggled to reconcile their sexuality with their culture and familial expectations would go to meet. There was a reason why some locals called it 'Effing Forest'.

The true boundaries of our forests are even more ancient than the royal perambulations and laws that in medieval times defined them. They are the limits of what we consider civilised and modern, and by crossing them I was leaving behind the rules of London, of how to behave in cities. For the man in the forest, this had allowed him to redefine life. I was desperate for it to do the same for me.

The first real sunshine of the year cracked the blinds of that central London hotel and woke us up early. I pretended to be asleep for a while, dreading the inevitable small talk about when we might meet again, but it ended up not being awkward at all. Two lives in crisis colliding for a few brief hours – that was all it was going to be. She took a cab back east and I the Overground to Chingford via the box room to get changed into sensible walking gear.

I walked slowly that afternoon, sapped of energy. I'd barely slept, and drifted off the main path to a patch of last year's leaves, not yet dried by the dappling sun. I lay down, the cool, soggy mulch soothing the aches of drinking and sex. The absence of any true intimacy the night before had left me feeling dislocated. Above me all was infinite and all was random, from the tiny buds to the patterns of the branches, the light that glanced off ridges on the bark. I imagined that I could be lying on the floor of any forest in the world. As I lay there I might die and be absorbed – the forest would not blink a moment but swallow up the nutrients locked inside me and carry on, uncaring and unknowing. I would be returned to the forest, to all of them, to the greatest power that the planet has ever seen and will ever know.

I stared up into the trees, hoping that the forest's embrace might calm and cradle me. But the limbs of the beeches, spreading out and thinning into twigs, were the capillaries, wrinkles and veins and the leaves the skin cells and creases of a giant, crushing palm. I was just a tiny bundle of proteins caught in their trap. My sorrow, my neuroses and fears were minuscule flickers of electricity.

Yet I already knew of one who had acceded to the universal through this place from which my family had come. The man who lived in the forest was in my Epping Forest story before I was even born, because his spirit has always existed and always will. I don't believe that any of us are ever that far away from a state of being that can turn us into complete outsiders. We've all got what it takes to jump off the path of convention and disappear into the thickets in search of our true, difficult selves. In the city, reality is just a veneer. With a forest so nearby, it's hardly surprising that so many use it to break that fragile cover.

3

Wreckers of Civilisation

On an overcast Sunday, humid for early March, the forest air was thick and faecal after days of heavy rain. I sweated uncomfortably through a buttoned-up shirt as I squelched up the hill from Chingford Plain, trying to stamp some purpose into my head. For every step I took, my wellies would slide another back through the oomska. I walked up towards Fairmead, a rising part of the forest where there was once an ancient oak, long since destroyed by vandals and fire. There was a hunting lodge there too, but no trace of it remains.

Towards the summit the woodland thins and a few wizardly old pollards dominate. Under one of them a family, religious group or something were gathered. With a hand-held camera they were filming a man stood against the trunk. He wore robes of rich orange, gold and red and on his head was perched a bright, tasselled, pot-shaped hat. He was surrounded by children, from toddlers up, all wearing circular wooden shapes in their hair. Off-camera a woman, also in elaborate robes, held her giggling baby over a bramble for a piss. I heard the man say something about a bag and start to chant, but at that moment – I hadn't noticed I'd slowed to a stop and was gawping – another man on the edge of the circle hissed at me, pointed at the camera and shooed me on, away from whatever this private ceremony was. I carried on towards the spire that rises just that little bit higher than the trees of Epping Forest.

High Beach Church, poking up above the distant horizon from the bedroom of that Walthamstow house, had been a totem, connecting the adult life I had been building near the forest with my family's history. It was then just an instinct, a half-thought not really based on all that much, I had always dreamed of having children with Alice and bringing them up here. Dad had always said that someone from the Turner line, an uncle perhaps, had been buried up in the church's graveyard. From the surrounding area came a family rumour that we were descended from the illegitimate son of a local aristocrat and his housekeeper. Many years before someone had brought up the story during a walk past Arabin House, a large mansion at High Beach, declaring that this was where our ancestor had worked, his illegitimate parentage meaning he was swiftly promoted through the ranks of the servants. Mum, always one to ignore signs that warned of a closed road, took no notice of the 'Strictly Private' boards nailed onto the fence. I remember the feel of her hands lifting me up to peer over at the house; I caught a glimpse of a white building immersed in foliage and people in the garden.

They shouted at us, Mum put me down and took my hand and we had to run.

Along with that furtive peek at the nearby house, High Beach Church had become lodged in my young mind by a picture my granny had painted of it at some point during her life. It'd been on the living-room wall for years. Unlike the other picture that obsessed me as a child, Granny's painting spoke of light and love, faith and security all combined in a spiritual home.

I used to spend hours on the sofa talking to Granny when she'd come to visit, and I still have the old-lady suitcase I used to lug up the stairs to her room, a memento of what she carried into my life. I learned a lot from her, about the forest and the community on her street, the night in 1940 when a family opposite went into their air-raid shelter and were obliterated by a direct hit. She talked of the forest just a few hundred yards away from this violence. Most of all she instilled in me a distrust of authority and rules, encouraging me to follow my own path, to not settle for anything less than I should. I wonder how much of this came from her own past. She would have loved to have been an art teacher, but her class and gender meant she had to leave school at fourteen to become a typist. She kept up the painting, however, and when we lived up in Yorkshire where I was born, Dad would take her on 'trips out' around the moors and dales, stopping off at art shows in church halls. He'd be mortified by Granny's habit of holding forth, in her ripping Essex foghorn tone that was pretty foreign in 1980s West Riding, on the failings of perspective, light and shade among her contemporaries in the pensioner art world. Granny's painting wasn't particularly outstanding, and had she exhibited it next to those depictions of chapels and purple hillsides and misshapen fruit, no doubt she'd have come in for the same excoriating criticism she herself meted out. The sky was blue, the trees were green, the church was brown, the graves little squares on a flat foreground and that was about it. Yet it was in her paintings, and especially that one of High Beach Church, that I so clearly felt her presence and personality.

High Beach isn't an especially remarkable building, but here in its own clearing, with the forest caressing its masonry and reaching over the low iron fence to over-hang the graves, it has a decidedly magical presence. The stones of the church emerge from the forest like rocks from a wave, the wash of branches and leaves flickering, dispersing to reveal it there, pale and silent against a landscape that roars all around.

For years I would always make sure that walks took in the church – a useful beacon, a halfway stop to the Woodbine pub on the far side of the forest, or a turning point at which to reverse back to the train at Chingford or Loughton. As I walked, the old children's rhyme would play over and over in my mind, the one you'd recite with complicated movements of the hands to make the shapes 'Here is the church and here is the steeple, open the door and here are the people.'

That day I sat on a bench by the locked church door feeling ill and tired, stomach churning old alcohol and indecision. Above me the clouds were a thick, heavy splodge, though it wasn't going to rain. No matter how hard I tried, I could not walk my way into my granny's painting, I could not connect my weary, dirty, sore self with the child, innocent and unspoiled.

It was from my parents that I'd inherited my love of Epping Forest. As a boy in the early 1950s Dad had attended Staples Road School, up a narrow alley from his home. The red-brick building has a white wooden bell tower capped with a weathervane and an elegant stepped chimney stack featuring a stone plaque on which is carved, 'Loughton Board School for Boys 1888'. It could be any school of the period, its architecture exuding progress for all and civic pride, were it not for the front yard, which is planted with evergreens, ivy and shrubs that reach across the quiet asphalt of Staples Road to the margins of the forest. From the road, a clearing rises up the slopes to some of the most ornate pollarded beeches of the forest, and during break-times pupils were allowed to play beneath them, so long as they didn't go over the crest of the hill.

Dad still has a school photo taken in that clearing, rows of serious, smartly dressed children set against the murk of the trees behind. Epping Forest was a diurnal presence in Dad's early life. He and my grandad would drag wood back for the open fires and central heating, and Granny would send him on missions to find moss for her hanging baskets, warning him to keep an eye out for keepers on the way back. Sometimes they'd see Jacob Epstein, the sculptor and local celebrity, flitting through the woodland. During the summer, Dad would have to walk through the forest to High Beach for swimming lessons in the outdoor pool behind the King's Oak pub.

Now it's a popular lido, the trees garishly illuminated at night, the water surrounded by hideous black and white loungers, tables and bar furnishings where the cast of *The Only Way Is Essex* like to flaunt abs, tans, tattoos and fake tits. Back in the 1950s, Dad loved to tell me, the walk through the trees would end with the scooping of dead snails, frogs and leaves from the unheated water before the class were made to plunge in.

Shortly after my dad enrolled at Staples Road School, another child walked through that doorway with 'Boys' spelled out in brick above the lintel. A photograph from the time shows Neil Megson in a deep V-neck jumper and tie, with large, intense eyes under a side parting and a smile that matches that gaze in being more devious than innocently mischievous. Years later, Megson would become Genesis P-Orridge, one of the founders of the art collective COUM and avant-garde music group Throbbing Gristle.

Throbbing Gristle had existed on the fringes of my imagination for years, but it was at a music festival in my early twenties that I encountered them for the first time. I still have the photograph I took during their set, bright light exploding from the ceiling and bouncing off Genesis' long, shock-blond hair like lightning. Out of the deep, solid, powerful thrum of the music blasted a cornet and snide, scratching vocals – a gruesome song about a burns victim – but there was life and a message in it that touched a nerve deep within me.

The Pontins holiday camp at Camber Sands, where the festival was taking place, was in fact a resonant place. The stage that Throbbing Gristle played on was in the same large venue that had been a frequent fixture in my childhood, when as a family we'd travel down for Dad to lead services at a Christian holiday week called Easter People. It had been a strange sensation at the time, feeling a deep connection with art, superficially so otherworldly and decidedly un-Christian, that was emanating from the same physical space where Dad delivered his sermons as a Methodist minister.

Dad was and remains a brilliant preacher and I have always found his words to be a source of inspiration and solace, not merely because I am his son. Yet as my mind was melting in front of Throbbing Gristle, I was acutely aware that what I was witnessing was very far from what I was supposed to be into – after all, I had a powerful memory of one of my relatives commenting that a sign for a cheesy nightclub called KISS on the outskirts of town might stand for 'Kids in Satan's Service'. Although Dad had introduced me to Leonard Cohen, the wider, sheltered, Christian world in which I had been brought up would panic in reaction to the supposedly evil power of amplified music and provocative art. As a teenager I'd leap up to turn down my stereo when I knew a particularly saucy lyric was imminent; I worried that liking a band called The Jesus and Mary Chain was in some way blasphemous, and Mum found all the swear words in my copies of the *NME* upsetting.

The Throbbing Gristle performance had stirred me up so much that I couldn't sleep that night, and instead of waiting for my mind to slow down enough for me to drop into unconsciousness, I ended up going for a dawn walk out past the barbed wire of the festival camp and onto Romney Marsh. A thick fog had drifted in from the sea. As I passed through the ghostly landscape barely able to see beyond my outstretched arms I had a fleeting vision that the rest of the world and the contradictions it imposed on me didn't exist. But I knew that it'd not be long before the sun burned the mist away.

Throbbing Gristle performed their first concert at the ICA in 1976. The event, called Prostitution, was the final retrospective of COUM Transmissions, an art collective founded in Hull by Genesis during the late 1960s. The visual art element of the event featured COUM and Throbbing Gristle member Cosey Fanni Tutti's work as a model in pornographic magazines and artefacts including her used tampons. Playing before a stripper and the punk band Chelsea in the main performance space, Throbbing Gristle debuted tracks with titles like 'Slug Bait' and 'Zyklon B Zombie'. The event provoked tabloid outrage – the *Sun* frothed that 'Mr Orridge is prostituting Britain' – and was debated in the House of Commons, with Conservative MP Nicholas Fairbairn thundering, 'It's a sickening outrage! Sadistic! Obscene! Evil! The Arts Council must be scrapped after this! These people are the wreckers of civilisation.'

Those last three words later became the title for the first book on COUM and Throbbing Gristle, which is where I discovered that Genesis P-Orridge and my dad had been to the same school on the edge of the woods that I loved. In *Wreckers of Civilisation*, Genesis is quoted as saying:

> Epping Forest was still untouched across the other
> side of the street . . . In the morning my mother would
> walk me to school. It took me about ten minutes
> through the forest along a trail worn by footsteps and
> deer. There were pools, frog ponds, deep shadows.
> It was a magical place, and also a favourite haunt, I
> learned later, for rapes, flashing, and the dumping of
> corpses.

Genesis would later name a track 'Epping Forest', a
haunting piece that reflects on a child's mind encountering the place for the first time somewhere on the other
side of innocence.

Dad had also mentioned the unsavoury side of the
forest, that at some point something had happened which
meant he and his classmates were no longer allowed
to go there unaccompanied. Yet for him and Mum it
remained not just a place of pastoral beauty but a living
memorial to God's creation. It was spiritually radical
too – they told me stories about religious meetings near
the forest in the 1960s, and of Gipsy Smith, the Romany
preacher who had been born in Epping Forest, the site
marked by a large stone.

How could Epping Forest have such a profound
impact on these young children, yet send them spiralling
off into such different directions? Perhaps they weren't
such different directions after all. In Vico's *The New
Science* the forest was the place of both barbarity and
the birth of reason. The very word 'forest' comes from

the Latin *foris* or *forestis*, meaning 'what is outside', especially the city gates. 'Savage' comes from *sylva*, the Latin for wood. The German word for forest, *Wald*, is thought to have the Indo-European origin meaning 'wilderness', and from a similar root, Chaucer in his *Canterbury Tales* uses both Middle English meanings of 'wood' – 'trees' and 'madness'. And there we are: 'root' – even the way we refer to our language is taken from the anchor of a tree. From *foris* we also derive 'foreign', while in the medieval period across Europe the wooded areas were outside the limits of the still-scattered human civilisations, and in them dwelled thieves, cut-throats, brigands, hermits, renegades, religious outcasts and other people of dubious repute who didn't fit in. My parents and Genesis P-Orridge, the children of the forest, were outsiders in their own different ways, taking from the landscape that had such an impact on their early years an understanding of the complex spirituality of society and self. They had found their own identities from the woods, but I was trapped between the trees and the city, not knowing which way to turn.

I had come to all this just at the time when I was starting to doubt my ability to continue to fit in, to continue doing what was expected of me. The ingrained confusion of bisexuality meant that I had long led a compartmentalised life, with the self I showed to friends and the one that I presented to my family in conflict. It had been too easy to live a secret, fragmented life, unknown to anyone except those I met within it. The temptation to slip into another furtive existence would always end up undermining the imagined future represented by that distant church tower.

It was clear too that what COUM and Throbbing Gristle had practised was a philosophy of challenging the self in order to uncover truths, a purer way of existing. I didn't find their work shocking – they represented a defiance of the norms I'd encountered throughout my life, the various quiet hypocrisies of a society that required binary living, the acceptance of specific roles in work, in behaviour, in sexuality. I could follow from their example, yet I still cherished the sacred truths that existed in the Bibles and hymnals behind the locked door of High Beach Church. By this point in my life, I had long thought, I should have resolved the doubts and confusions that during teenage years had slithered up to strangle the happy child. I hadn't.

As I sat on the bench in the graveyard in the clearing in the middle of Epping Forest, I knew that if I'd come here looking for a signal as to which way I should turn for resolution I wasn't going to find it. The church was silent. Another airliner above whined down into London. It was a windless day and the trees were still, weighing on me as heavily as the turgid sky as I picked myself up and started back towards Chingford.

I tried to find the family who looked so happy, so immersed in their ritual, so I could ask them why they were there and what truths they might have discovered. But I couldn't work out the way back to that old oak. I didn't have a map and I'd been so busy on the repetitive swipe'n'type of my dating apps that my phone had run out of battery. Lost and frustrated, I stumbled along through the woods, not knowing or really caring where

I was. In the distance I could hear the motorway and around me the usual sounds of the forest, but I couldn't use them for guidance.

A giant tree had cracked down the middle and fallen in two directions, as cleanly as a log split by an axe. I jumped up onto the middle of the stump to try and get a view out of the clearing and immediately sank over my shoes into stinking rotten wood. Feeling like an idiot, I stomped on.

Ahead a darker, snaking strip showed black against the forest floor in the crepuscular gloom. As I approached, I saw it was the Ching brook, flowing thick and the colour of gravy after the heavy rain. I remembered something that Dad had told me. If I was ever to lose my way through the forest I shouldn't just keep going, as the formless woodland would force me into walking in circles. He told me to find running water and follow it downstream, for it'll always lead me to safety. I traced the sluggish, winding current of the Ching down to the edge of the plain and then across it, over to the station, eager to wash away the deathly forest and dive once more into the distractions of the city night.

4

Two Camps

The decision to dynamite the foundations of a life will always throw rubble in unexpected directions. The emotional wrench of ending a five-year relationship was bad enough, but I hadn't thought through the practicalities. London had changed drastically in the years since I'd last had to look for a room to rent. I couldn't escape the anxiety-triggering realisation that fast-rising rents across London meant that I was going to struggle to afford to live anywhere half decent. I endlessly searched online ads offering ugly divan beds in corners that would give a feng-shuist a minor stroke for hundreds of pounds a month more than I could afford.

In any case, I was rather enjoying staying with my friends in the box room of their Walthamstow house, even though it appeared to be falling down around us. Shortly after they bought it they broke up, but they were still both living there. I adopted a sort of UN role, paying my way with dinners and long conversations, late into the night. After the radiators were removed we'd sit on the old sofa hugging an electric heater, ploughing our way through any booze we could find in the house.

The Walthamstow streets that spread towards Epping Forest were built fast and speculatively in the nineteenth century – the local artisan designer and writer William Morris rather snobbishly described the developments that approached his home as 'hideous brick encampments'. Like my friends' house, many went up without proper foundations and just bare earth beneath the floorboards. These modest two-and-a-half-up-and-down homes might now be worth three-quarters of a million quid on some streets, but, with a whistle through pursed lips and a shake of his head, a builder told me that many of them are only really propped up by the house next door. This place was no exception.

In the years since the houses were constructed, meddling DIY enthusiasts and dubious practitioners of the building trade hadn't helped matters. A previous occupant had removed the downstairs chimney breasts but not the fireplaces or flue upstairs, meaning that tonnes of brick were supported by just a few floorboards. A bathroom had been added at the back, but without its breeze blocks being tied into the rest of the house it was now falling off. The entire place was riddled with dry and wet rot, and all the plaster and ceilings had been taken down, covering everything in a layer of grey dust. The arguments of the large family next door buzzed through the walls. One day the endless rows, words inaudible but intent entirely clear, ceased for a singing of 'Happy Birthday'. Seconds after the final refrain, the angry voices resumed with increased ferocity.

I was doing my best to put a brave face on things – years of Methodist socialism had drummed into me that I ought to be grateful for what I had; but the feeling of impermanence was starting to eat away at me. I was living out of two suitcases, and my possessions were still at Alice's place fifteen minutes up the road. Cut off from that Epping Forest view from her bedroom, I now looked out only onto a bathroom roof and the unkempt gardens of the houses at the back.

Home is such a basic human instinct that even my position of privilege that I had a roof over my head was making me feel unhealthily removed from a belief in my own future. My enthusiasm for doing anything except hunting the affirming red dots of social media – Facebook likes, Tinder matches, the Grindr buzz – was starting to make it hard to believe there was much point in getting up off that grotty mattress in the morning.

I still felt the impulse to visit the forest, but ever since that frustrating walk to High Beach the trees had lost their power. It was the man who lived somewhere in it who drew me there now. From our first meeting I felt that he was on a different plane of consciousness from anyone else I knew. You could see it in those eyes, hear it in the way he spoke, bolstered by the wisdom that comes with no longer caring what anyone else thinks about you or where you come from. I was sensitive to the fact that it might be hard to get him to speak about how he'd ended up making his home in Epping Forest, but he had no reservations about talking. Perhaps when you have consciously welcomed death, the gags of self-restraint and censorship are broken.

Again his rich scent filled the kitchen of the living room in my aunty and uncle's house opposite the trees, a ghost made of ancient woodland air that had just slipped across the tarmac. The clock chimed, warm and brassy, as the man who lives in the forest began to speak. His accent was a curious one, a mix of rural burr and Essex twang. In our conversations he held my gaze, turning away only once or twice with a sharp jerk of his head, usually when he'd found something amusing. Those eyes never dimmed or watered, no matter how difficult his story became.

He'd held down tough jobs that had forced him to face claustrophobia, loneliness, physical extremes, struggles with authority and violence. There were relationships, but what was eventually diagnosed as bipolar disorder worsened steadily and they ended. There were spells in psychiatric institutions. The breaking point had come when he was about to be evicted from his flat for non-payment of council tax. 'My son told me I should pay my tax, everyone has to otherwise it's anarchy,' he explained. 'I said to him, "I've been a soldier, sailor, rich man, poor man, beggar man, why not be an anarchist too?"' He let rip a staccato laugh, revealing a full, straight set of small teeth.

Upon notice of his eviction he had stopped taking his medication, believing it would lead to such an abominable state of mind that it'd be easier for him to take his own life. He presented his decision with such impeccable logic that I found myself nodding along. I'd accepted his conviction that there was no better option – a court case, a spell in another psychiatric hospital where he felt like a prisoner and had no friends, aside from one teenage Muslim girl who had tried to commit suicide. Knowing that dead weight is harder to remove than even the angriest man, he took a dog lead and climbed onto the chair. Yet he couldn't take that step. Something stopped him that day. Instead, he got down off the chair, opened the front door of his flat for the final time, and started walking.

It was a Saturday and he had three quid in his pocket until he could withdraw his next pension. He bought three pasties that would last him for three days. He found some cardboard behind Tesco Express, a plastic bag to make a jacket tied with two pebbles and a snotter knot, and stuffed newspaper up his jumper. For a while he slept in the lychgate of Theydon Bois Church, a small wooden structure framed by two giant oaks, one pollarded and half a millennium old, the other thought to have been planted around the time of the church's construction in the nineteenth century. Those two trees were his gateposts to the forest. One night, as he lay asleep under a plastic sheet in the lychgate he was attacked by strangers. Punched, kicked and stamped on. With his arthritis he couldn't fight back, though he'd certainly have liked to. When the attack was over and he had recovered some strength, he picked himself up and walked between those two sentinel trees, retreating into the folds of Epping Forest.

I wasn't sure if he had chosen the forest or it had chosen him. It certainly provided for him: he found a tent, left by some kids who had taken a cheap, disposable self-erecting device of the kind popular at music festivals into the woods and were too lazy to repack it. For a while he kept moving, pitching camp across the forest, even sleeping in the middle of Ambresbury Banks, the undulating ramparts of what used to be an Iron Age fort rumoured to have been the place where the Queen of the Iceni fought her last stand against the Romans. Of all the places he could have chosen to sleep, something had drawn him here. 'They say that Boudica wasn't there, that she didn't have her battle,' he told me. 'Well I know. She was there.'

As he spoke, it occurred to me that, far from being crazy, the man in the forest might be living the life of Riley. With his pension and no rent to pay, he had a far greater disposable income than most people I knew living down in London, just ten miles away according to the nearest milestone on Epping New Road. At Christmas people left money for him in the local shop, but he asked that it be given to charity. He refused gifts of food, politely explaining that he'd already had his daily pastry with a Costa coffee from the machine in Tesco. He seemed quite the connoisseur of the different green teas available in local cafés and enthused about the health benefits of Manuka honey. For breakfast he might have a tin of beans, raw garlic and some olives, and then not really eat for a day or two. 'The animals living around me don't cook, do they?'

He'd dropped in that day on the way to buy the *Independent*, the only newspaper he trusted. Sometimes, he told me, he'd order books from the local bookshop, though he wasn't a fan of fiction, apart from one writer – he enthused at length about Hilary Mantel's *The*

Assassination of Margaret Thatcher. He said he liked happy endings. He could recite passages of Thomas Hood's poetry, including 'The Epping Hunt'. He sat up straight in his chair: 'Epping,' he pronounced, 'for butter justly famed, and Pork in sausage popp'd'. The line set off another dry, rattling chuckle. He told me that he loved to laugh. Sometimes a passage from a book would have him rolling around his camp in stitches, despite the arthritis that made it hard for him to get back up again.

He liked to follow politics and wasn't afraid to share his views, which seemed to be a sort of socially conscious left-leaning libertarian anarchism. They didn't appear to have anything to do with his decision to live in the forest, which I am still not convinced was ever a conscious decision at all. He had ended up living off-grid merely because that's where his mind led him.

Our tea long finished, the man in the forest said he wanted to get his paper and head off to read in one of his favourite places – Village View. Many of the well-appointed suburban dwellings around these parts have names like Forest Side, Forest Edge or Forest View, and I liked his inversion of the norm. I pictured him sitting there, trees behind him, looking at the sensible suburban lives passing by, and wondered what he thought of them all.

We parted on the Forest ride and I walked back to the Central Line to Leytonstone, and the 158 bus that meandered up Blackhorse Road, then Blackhorse Lane, and the turning off to my box room. My key was stiff in the front door (something to do with the weight of the house pushing down on the frame and sending it wonky) and, tired by the walk and the cold outside, I nodded off in the bare-brick living room. At some point while I snoozed my flatmate and her new girlfriend (things had moved on after she'd broken up with the boyfriend with whom she part owned the house) got home. They were still in the early flushes of love and took every opportunity at home or in the museum, pub or art-gallery toilet cubicles of London to express this with the exertions of fingers and tongues. I don't think they'd realised that the removal of ceiling plaster meant that there was nothing to dampen the volume between floors – there was one gap large enough to pass a cup of tea through – and I was often woken by moans and thumps from upstairs.

I'm not really the sort to be offended by the sound of people fucking (I'm not the sort to be aroused by it either, it's more sweet and charming to me than any-thing else), but I didn't want them to feel bad and it was slightly distracting as, half asleep, I tried to put myself in the mindset of the man from the forest. It was no good. I took out my phone and opened Facebook. A friend married to a woman from Romania who had developed a strong bond and affection for the country had been spending the last few days using his profile to share a running commentary on the events of the revo-lution that toppled the Communist dictatorship in 1989. He'd reached 21 December, when Nicolae Ceauşescu addressed 80,000 of his people from a balcony of the Communist Party headquarters. My friend had shared YouTube footage shot by the state television channel for what was intended as a broadcast to rally the people behind their leader. A cry slipped through the floor-boards above me as Ceauşescu's wooden, rasping voice butted against the crowds, whose cheers soon became jeers. I increased the volume on my laptop, sending a quacking noise echoing around the room with each push of the button, and watched the horror spread across the face of the dictator as he rapped the microphone as if suspecting a faulty line, and pleaded with the crowd to calm down. Another wail and a squeak from upstairs and I put my headphones on as Ceauşescu left his balcony. I saw but didn't hear the rattle of dry mortar from the bottom of the precarious chimney.

5

The House That Silenced the City

We trace patterns across the city, running energy from our interactions along trails of microscopic particles, hair and skin cells, a slipstream invisible to anything save the microbes and mites that feed on us. Much as we might ascribe sentiment to a place, none except the most magical can transform from brick and concrete, plaster and glass into light. Sometimes, though, a quiet spell can be cast in the most ordinary spots by a kindly soul.

It wasn't long before the demolitions meant that the Walthamstow house became entirely uninhabitable and I had to move out of the box room. Friends again came to my assistance, offering me a bed in a house further west, away from the forest in Tottenham: 147 Tower Gardens Road, a red-brick temple of respite hiding behind a privet hedge. It was kept under the munificent watch of Ian Johnstone, artist, permaculturalist and spiritual thinker. Ian was another connection to the world I encountered with Throbbing Gristle all those years ago. He was once the partner of Jhon Balance who, with Throbbing Gristle's Peter 'Sleazy' Christopherson, had formed the band Coil. Over two decades of the kind of operational intensity few have managed since, Coil's music undertook a gradual shift from rugged carnality to a more sensuous, spiritual period they described as a 'moon phase'. Over the years I had become obsessed by their music and how it sounded like man dissolving into nature. Narcotic and queer, it blurred the boundaries between our expectations of sonic urbanism and the pastoral psychedelic.

Although I had heard that the relationship between Coil and extended members of their curious world had been turbulent, and when Balance died after a drunken fall in 2004 it soured murkily, the whispers could do nothing to detract from the energy of that house. It was exactly what I needed. The two big brass cocks sitting pride of place in Ian's old room might have tarnished, but they were still hard.

To Ian, 147 Tower Gardens Road was more than the rented house in which he lived. In repeated acts of kindness, he opened its suburban door to many who, beaten down by exhausted love in an increasingly cold and gilded city, had nowhere else to go. At the time he was living with his boyfriend in Spain, where they were trying to turn a ruined village on the edge of forest and city into a centre for organic, holistic, horticultural education, and needed someone to keep an eye on his London home.

I had never lived alone before, but here I instantly felt at ease. It was a quiet and strange place that conjured an ancient, magical wilderness right into the heart of one of the toughest parts of the city. Inside, Ian had built shelves, tables, cupboards and platforms for beds out of wood, and stained everything, including the floorboards, a rich, dark brown. There were no doors, just curtains hung in the doorframes, and the bath was hidden behind a glass cabinet which, if you peered very closely, was home to a set of tiny figurines that might have wandered lost from a train set to be trapped for ever in a Lilliputian prison. Scattered about the place were books, disco wigs, two sculpted silver deer-leg plinths that he'd used in a performance once. The loo was flushed with an old rusty chain, and in the stairwell a wooden chimney reached up through the roof to a skylight that could trap the moon. The walls were hung with unusual, some said magically potent paintings by the little-known Edwardian artist Austin Osman Spare. There were two canvases in my room, one showing fantastical creatures, rodents and amphibians from a peculiar dream, while at the other end of the wooden bed platform was a portrait of a goddess in green and gold. I had met a woman who was also attempting to reconcile a religious upbringing with sexual curiosity and for a while we were blissfully happy, spending days exploring the secret recesses of each other's imaginations as much as our bodies. I watched her naked against the sunlight on that wall, her skin glowing in the green light through the window. It was as if the creature in that painting had come alive to wrap her legs round me.

The filtering of the light from outside was Ian's

greatest creation, as if he had command of the sun and the cold and the noise of the city. The neighbours' gardens were in varying levels of cultivation or dereliction, and Ian had planted the small patch of land that led onto the park behind with twisted willow, acer, irises, ceanothus, papery white peonies and a bay. Ivy had completely covered the back of the house, crowding in over my bedroom window as if it were camouflaging the entrance to a cave. A few stems had crept through a crack in the window and I slept in that room like I had never slept before. I'd awaken to the rustling of a dunnock flapping in its roost against the glass by my head as night melted away from the leaves of the ivy, turning them from black to dark green, my room the same colour as the nest of the bird.

Around this menagerie, Tottenham got on with its business loudly, the buses sloughing up the old Roman road, now the A10. Walking was a better way of getting around, through Lordship Rec where every day a hundred black crows patrolled the grass. A stygian river emerged from a culvert to snake through an incongruous wild-flower meadow for a few hundred yards, stinking bubbles of decay bursting its surface to prickle against the sky. To close the door of 147 behind me after this stygian crossing was to be willingly consumed by an orb of must and mould, dust and greenery, and, above all, peace. In the garden it was as if London no longer existed, with nobody to converse with save an old stone frog and the muttering willow leaves, the melodic plink of water into metal bowls under the ivy. That drip never ceased, even when it was hot and rain had stayed away, and I would sit naked on the back porch underneath the ivy and listen to its song.

Though I was enjoying the isolation, the convoluted route of public transport meant that it was hard to reach the forest. I made the effort when my aunty called and told me that the man in the forest was keen to take me up to his camp. Our initial meetings had gone well, but I wasn't sure if he would be willing to let me visit a place that few people around the forest had seen unless they'd accidentally stumbled upon it. Even then, they'd quickly forget where it was, and on one of the occasions when he hadn't been spotted on his Costa perambulation for a few days, concerned search parties could sweep the area but find no trace.

'How've you been?' I asked, wondering if he'd been affected by a recent cold snap. 'Just the job,' he declared enthusiastically. 'They said in London it was minus one but at ground level I can assure you it does drop lower. If I can leave the bottle of olive oil at forty-five degrees but the fluid level remains where it was ... I'm thinking I might make some sort of scale for temperature depending on where the oil is.'

As we chatted about his plans for making an amateur thermometer we started the trudge down into Genesis Slade, on the other side of the road from my uncle and aunty's house. He wore a solid pair of walking boots, waterproof trousers, a black shirt and a fleece that zipped into a raincoat. A Swiss Army knife hung on a lanyard round his neck. He told me that he'd recently made a cape out of bin bags. 'They say these bags will last for a thousand years. Well I won't!' That laugh again. The trick to a successful bin-bag cape, he told me as we walked, is not to cut anything, just to fold. He even had a perfect bin-bag cowl, looking like a monk making a cameo appearance in a *Mad Max* film. He kept his supplies – and perhaps a few valuables, though he denied he had any – in two carrier bags. One was slung across his back, the other tied at the top with a pencil stuck through the knot. Rather cleverly, this then hooked into the string from the other bag over his chest, meaning the weight was balanced across his body, helpful given the discomfort he felt from a shoulder broken in a motorcycle accident.

I admired his innovations, from the blueprint for the radical new olive-oil thermometer to these expertly engineered bits of hiking gear. I'm fairly sure that, stuck in some apocalyptic scenario where I had to fend for myself, I'd not manage nearly so well. He was certainly much better at it than the bronzed and buff types that end up marooned on desert islands on reality television programmes. With my nylon rucksack and everything bought off the shelf at Cotswold Leisure, I felt rather inadequate beside him.

Despite his slow, swinging gait, he walked with a quiet confidence towards his home through a late-winter morning that tasted of mildew. Off piste, on piste, across a stream and climbing higher. By then I'd learned enough about his past life to know that if he wanted to, he could deliberately have led me on this circuitous route to ensure I'd never find him again. But then it could be a trick of my mind. In the forest it's hard to know what path you're on.

I'd been following my own camping logic, expecting to find that he'd set up in a pleasant clearing, perhaps on a forest rise, a stream babbling just far enough away not to flood his place. For him, aesthetics weren't so much of a concern. We came upon his tent all of a sudden in one of the densest parts of the forest, not terribly well hidden in the lee of a holly thicket. Unlike the messes made by your everyday forest campers who, with their fires, bright torches, loud music and litter, might as well have stayed at home and had a party in their living room, his camp was scrupulously clean and tidy. A few bent beech saplings supported his main tent and there was a second flysheet over the top. Attached to one of the boughs that held up his tent was a clear plastic bag containing a note on a scrap of paper simply showing his name and the words 'In Use'.

His improvised home, built from what nature offered and what others had left behind, reminded me of a photograph I'd seen, dating from the turn of the last century, of 'The Epping Forest Hermit and His Camp'. It shows an old boy who looks much like the man from the forest, in stout boots, jacket, hat and white beard, sat with his stick in the doorway of a domed structure covered in foliage and ferns. I suspect the figure in the photograph is William Burke, who lived near Great Monk Wood in Loughton. He told a local historian that he had a 'good reading', and word was that he had left society behind after a deep love went awry. Young men would go and visit him in the forest on a Sunday in search of wisdom and advice in exchange for tobacco, books and breakfast until, after a cold spell, he died of pneumonia and was buried at Loughton Church.

Every village and woodland in England would once have had a few characters like William Burke and, as Oliver Rackham put it, 'no forest was really complete without a hermit'. Epping Forest was also home to Henry Plodden, an unemployed carpenter who lived in a hollow tree in 1905, while the *Woodford Times* reported that a man called Charles Sheridan lived in a bush for thirty years. It wasn't just men, either. The Kate of Kate's Cellar, a valley that bolsters the ramparts of the Iron Age Loughton Camp, was either a nineteenth-century hermit or a fourteenth-century witch, depending on which Chinese whisper of local history you want to believe. Kind Kitty 'had a cultured voice and I think had been quite a lady ... considerate and kind ... dirty but not coarse', as one local testimony had it. These nomads could wander the countryside in times before local authorities and landowners clamped down and started moving people on. I wonder if in modern society the raising of many millions of people from a life that always risked teetering on the edge of poverty and homelessness has made us more callous and unsympathetic towards those who seem to have made a choice of the hermit life. Over the centuries, many thousands have been forced to make their home in Epping Forest through sheer poverty, and there are plenty of accounts of out-of-work men who tramped through, sleeping in a different spot each night, much as George Orwell described in *Down and Out in Paris and London*. Historically, it's not hard to feel that a dry shelter under a tree, taking charity from passers-by, was preferable to the workhouse, but this isn't even a thing of the past.

Although I was being buffeted by the growing London crisis, my own situation was nothing compared to the many people, frequently immigrants, who couldn't even find a toehold in the subdivided houses or garages of the capital's new slum landlords. Down on Wanstead Flats you increasingly come across rough shelters of cardboard, a few sleeping bags, eyes watching warily from a nearby bench. Yet it feels as though there's a strange class system among the forest dwellers. We find the hermits fascinating, but turn a blind, uncharitable eye towards the desperate. Why is that? In a time when governments reinforce a mantra of 'strivers versus shirkers', those down in the forest's more urban southern end might seem like an eyesore, an inconvenience. Perhaps Burke, Plodden, Sheridan, Kate, Kind Kitty or the man in the forest are tolerated because deep down we all know that anyone's mind can rewire itself. Sometimes the realities of life put too much strain on the ties that keep us harnessed to work, home and relationships, and it breaks them. These aren't people who've chosen to get away from it all in imitation of Thoreau, heading to his log cabin on the banks of Walden Pond. They will not be using the #cabinporn hashtag on Instagram, virtue-signalling a smug rejection of modernity in the pompous endpoint of our fallacious contemporary view of nature as an escape from the urban way of life. For them the forest fulfils a visceral need, providing a home because it asks no questions and demands nothing in return.

The zip on the door of the tent had frayed away from the nylon material, but neat loops had been sewn in place to keep it shut. He suggested I open the door: 'I can't get in and out too easy, but you have a look inside.' There was no groundsheet; the camp bed that he slept on rested on bare forest earth. At the back of the tent was a pile of books, but that was it; no camping stove or anything like that. I was slightly surprised by the absence of any kind of smell. In England we are, after all, obsessed with toilets. My aunty had said that there was a bit of an ammonia whiff to the man in the forest's camp, but I couldn't really detect anything, just the damp scent of the forever-rotting woodland.

Reversing backwards out of the tent, I told him how much I liked his camp, pitched where it was in Epping Forest for who knows what reason his mind had chosen. '"You live like an animal", someone told me,' he said. 'Yes! It's lovely! The foxes I give chicken to, they don't tell me I smell.' Unfortunately, after complaints about an earthy pong, he was banned from going into one half of a local pub. He seemed quite amused by this, as the forbidden zone is the dog bar where labradors, spaniels and so on are permitted after a forest walk. 'If I wanted a drink I'd have to send a dog in to get me a pint,' he said with a salvo of laughs. 'One lady told me I smell a bit between a horse and a fox. I loved that.'

He did wash sometimes, rinsing himself as rain fell through the trees, and afterwards like a citizen of ancient Rome rubbed his body with olive oil. He was once offered a bottle of eau de cologne to mask his whiff but turned it down, saying that his desire to go for a drink in a local boozer wasn't strong enough for him to want to mask the signature *parfum* of his life in the forest. 'They call it drowning your sorrows,' he said. 'Well I ain't got none.' I laughed and told him that I needed to go and drown mine, but stopped myself before I could tell him why. I didn't want to burden him with what I thought must sound like trivial concerns, even though they were shaking me to the core. I told him I ought to be going, and asked the best way to the Green Ride and Epping Station. He pointed through the bushes and said I'd not miss it. He was right: after a few seconds pushing through the holly and saplings I found myself on the main ride through the forest. His secret camp wasn't as secluded as I'd assumed it might be. I turned on the gravel track and faced the trees. There was no sign he even existed, or ever came this way.

I started the long, convoluted journey back to my own green refuge. The intensity of the new connection in my life hadn't been enough to make it endure against the shredded wounds of the past. Instead it had created tensions that refused to ease, no matter what chemistry was borne over our bodies, and at its most beautiful and extreme it was as if we were turning each other inside out. In fact, it just made it all worse. Familiar feelings of guilt and stranger desires had started to return. I'd closed off and she finished it with a curt email. I settled back into my solitary life in the room with the window covered in ivy, my own forest in the heart of the city. But my brief experience of peace within it wasn't to last.

One night, wandering deep in the vast landscape of sleep, I was woken by the stroke of a hand on my face.

My eyes opened to see a figure crouching over me, lit by the pale-green dawn through the window. 'Who's this then?' the bearded man asked. I blinked and he vanished. I was awake. I was fully aware. I was not afraid. The birds started to sing again and after a short while lying there, feeling an odd but peaceful atmosphere in the room, I drifted off back into sleep.

The next day I wanted to speak to Daniel, a musician and dear friend of Ian's who had arranged for me to move into the house. I thought that he, a deeply curious and spiritual person, would want to hear about this unusual apparition, but I couldn't get hold of him. In the early afternoon a Facebook message arrived from a mutual pal. 'Are you at Tower Gardens? Have you heard the news? Is everything OK?' What news, I asked. 'Ian died last night.' That strange calm I'd felt in the early hours washed back over me. Although he'd allowed me into his home, Ian had never met me. The figure that had touched my face – well, I knew what Ian looked like. Something of the magic of that place seemed to have brought him back, just for a moment, to say goodbye to it.

When any life ends it leaves behind the strangest jetsam, the drawers of safety pins and string, piles of books that'll remain unread, socks never to be reunited with their pairs, wholesale sacks of basmati rice. There was a memorial afternoon for Ian in the house that silenced the city, quiet words and tears in the garden next to the stone frog, but none of us had been present when his earthly form departed. It was as if he had disappeared into a Spanish woodland.

The rooms emptied quickly, dust unsettled in angry eddies. It would not be long before I was on the move again, and I'm glad I didn't see the destruction of what had been so lovingly created there.

The garden has gone now, ripped up, destroyed, turned to smoke atop a municipal pyre. No doubt coat after coat of beige paint was applied to try and cover the dark, warm wood inside, and the ivy has been ripped from the brickwork. Ian Johnstone's brass cocks, paintings and silver deer legs were scattered to the winds. 147 Tower Gardens was not merely a home in a storm and a haven in a grasping city, but a hermitage, a refuge made of wood and of the woods. It was a place so special that its very existence and my time in it quickly started to feel like a dream, for death would not leave me during the months of that early spring.

6

The Understorey

Through the wet windows of the Golden Fleece pub I could see the blurred forms of people in awkwardly fitting black suits and dresses huddled under umbrellas, trying to scratch flames out of damp lighters. Behind them, the rain drifted over Wanstead Flats like a sheet of gauze, washing the colours of April out of the grass and emerging leaves that were not yet scattered thickly enough for new life to glow through the weather.

I was having lunch with Mum and Dad after the funeral of Granny's best friend, Edie, who'd died just a couple of weeks after Ian's memorial. We weren't part of any of the wakes in the pub, which lent a curious air of detachment as we sat eating fish and chips and talking about family. The conversation among the mourners was muted but urgent. At a wake the tributes and condolences to friends and relatives you'll not see again until the next one have to be just so. There were quiet laughs and choked sobs around a table covered in photographs, black and white and worn through the ages alongside rough colour printouts from phone cameras. A group from a different wake occupied a separate corner, G&Ts, glasses of wine and pints of lager occasionally being raised in toast. Though we were all strangers from different funerals, the rooms of the pub had a quiet mood of togetherness, for we'd all left someone just over the way, where the drizzle dampened the flowerbeds of the City of London Cemetery.

Although she was well into her nineties when she died, on my final visit with Dad to see Edie she'd talked of her boyfriend, 'a young fella in his seventies'. There is a photo of her and Granny on the streets in Leyton from way back, before they became part of the great twentieth-century movement of East Enders from inner London to Essex. Husbands came and went, but those two were inseparable. Edie always kept a room in her bungalow in Potters Bar which she called 'Dorrie's room'. There was an intensity to their friendship that I am not sure we see so often in this faster-moving, more transitory age. I'd wanted to be there for Edie and for Dad, who had the difficult task of conducting the burial service in the place where his own parents had been laid to rest.

I'd nearly made us late for the service, overly trusting my phone's satnav against Dad's local knowledge of the roads to the cemetery. He'd been understandably annoyed with me, but that hadn't impacted on the quiet tenderness of his sermon for the members of Edie's family, gathered in one of the small chapels that sit in the rich landscaping of the cemetery, as verdant as an arboretum. There's an exultancy to how it's planted, the trees and thick shrubberies a distraction from the functional aspects of these places, concealing the furnace chimneys and the next fleet of black cars waiting round the corner to take their slot. It's in these municipal spaces that the quiet words for the departing are like birdsong in the trees surrounding; a gentle ease.

We're changed for ever the first time someone close to us dies. If the earliest taste of love is a heady yet sickening awareness of our instinct to share ourselves, then the shock of bereavement lifts the trapdoor that covers a totality of absence that we know we will have to face again and again. Love evolves with knowledge and with the different people we share it with and, if we are fortunate, might carry us through to a place of happiness. Grief does not – its truth is absolute, for in it we see our own end.

Just as, a few weeks before, the loss of Ian had broken the spell of 147 Tower Gardens, so now Edie's funeral had taken me back to summer 1997 when Granny, then in her eighties but seemingly in good health and with her personality undimmed, had suffered an aneurysm and died in the course of an afternoon. Both Mum and Dad had lost parents young and were not afraid of discussing it openly. Death was, after all, part of Dad's work, and belonging to a church community meant that funerals were common. Neither was death itself something to be feared, for the Christian faith offered the promise of an eternal afterlife.

Yet this was different. Granny was such a strong presence in my life and, in her exhortations to mistrust hierarchy and 'not be a bluestocking like so-and-so's grandchild', an inspiration. Ian's passing, and now Edie's, had brought back the strange momentum that death, the ultimate stopping, has: the knowing, the life being hit sideways, the swiftness of plans being made, the tears heard through floors and at the other end of the phone and then there you are, in the back of a funeral car.

Granny's funeral had taken place in Loughton's Methodist Church, a modern, glass-fronted building on the high street. I don't remember much about the specifics, just echoes of the accepting defiance of the joyous hymns and the light after we followed the coffin out of the church. The brightness of that day was odd. As we struggled in our grief, the people of Loughton going about their daily routine seemed alien, popping into the shops that Granny would talk about. It crowded my mind with memories of tiny details of her life that were heartbreaking now they had died with her. Her shopping trips to Superdrug and Safeway, Scrabble matches with the people at the end of the terrace, and Toch H – I never fully understood what it was but it seemed like a secret society for brooch-wearing ladies of a pensionable age.

What I especially remember from that day was the drive down to the City of London Cemetery. The view from the back of a funeral car offers a particular insight into how we deal with death: some people turn away as if they've seen the shadow of their own future pass before them, others gawp or attempt a respectful nod. We moved down from the High Road through Buckhurst Hill and into Woodford, and if I travel that route on the number 20 bus today the flashes of memory are still vivid, as if families employed photographers at funerals as well as weddings. I picture the cars moving round a corner, craning my neck to see the one with Granny in it in her box, which didn't look like real wood at all but was the colour of aspirational kitchen cabinets. Even now, a recollection of the smell of her tiny kitchen is triggered – gas and coal and sliced hard-boiled eggs for lunch, the light-green 1940s Woods Ware crockery, the hatch through to the sitting room where it opened out above Kulu Goi, a carved wooden head with two left hands that Grandad had supposedly brought back from the war and of which I used to be afraid.

The car drove down further into Woodford to the very edge of the forest. It all looked so unfamiliar, not the dense beech pollarded woodland with the brown-mulch carpet and holly understorey just a few minutes' walk from the home where Granny had been taken ill and in which Dad and my uncle had grown up. A bright-red sign, 'Beware of cattle', the burr of the grid under the wheels that seemed so at odds with a city funeral. The grass of Wanstead Flats was a lake of gold, the summer's day lit up the ornate gatehouse of the cemetery and crematorium. I don't recall anything else, just sadness that the truth that she was gone was the first unquestionable absolute I had really known.

In the distant past, many of our number would have died in the forests, their bodies left to be absorbed into the ground. There is something reassuring about the idea of returning to the forest in death. A decaying corpse sends nutrients into the soil that are picked up by the roots of the trees to burst into leaves from the skeletal twigs in springtime. The association of death and the forest is part of who we are. In *The New Science*, Vico points out that the etymology of 'human' is bound up with burial, *humanus* is man, *humus* the ground. In modern English 'humus' is the decayed plant and animal life that forms the forest floor. Now the dead are removed from the forests; bodies are found, a coroner is called, a black zipped-up bag transports the physical form from the bright byre of the woodland.

Forests are giant carpets of death, trillions of leaves rotting down to soil, the fallen forms of old trees, the slimy and fetid remnants of decaying fungi, the bones of animals ripped apart by scavengers leaving lonely skulls winking up from the mulch, ready to be collected by walkers and taken home as ornaments. I know that the man in the forest fully intended to die there too, just not by his own hand. He would not have wanted to be removed, but in death he would have had no opportunity to protest.

It is through the dead that we see how lives changed our forests. In a file in the London Metropolitan Archives is a black and white photograph of what appears to be a rotting log. The wood is black, old, hollowed. It is photographed in isolation, not against the broken debris of the forest floor but the solid grey background of somewhere indoors. The eye is drawn to lighter forms and something long and thick running alongside the wood, shorter pieces at right angles. It's an old picture, rudely copied, but upon a closer look that longer shape becomes a human thigh bone and the shorter one, ribs. It is a photograph of an early Bronze Age inhumation that took place in the Lee Valley just below the forest around 2,000 years ago. The burial was disinterred during the late 1930s by work to build reservoirs for creeping suburban London's water supply at Chingford, and removed to the then London Museum in Kensington for study. His wander beyond the grave didn't last long: a couple of years after its exhumation the coffin and skeleton met an unceremonious end, blown to pieces by German bombs during the Blitz. Wood and bone crushed together, incinerated, a second funeral and an unbidden cremation.

The forest has hidden bodies ever since, in the churchyard at High Beach where Dad's rumour had it an ancestor was buried, in St John's Churchyard on the edge of Loughton where I'd seen my maternal grand-father buried in the same grave as my mum's mother, who I never knew. A blue plaque marks that graveyard as the final resting place of Thomas Willingale, a man without whom the forest as we know it today would not exist.

Without the City of London Cemetery, where my granny and grandad and Edie and almost a million east Londoners have been interred down in the southern end of the forest in Wanstead, Epping Forest would not have survived either. It was death and vice that made the saving of it possible, and defined the boundary of the place I had become obsessed with. As I was increasingly finding on my trawls through the forest archives, death and sex have shaped and saved it, however deep into the past you might like to go. It is not and has never been a place of sylvan innocence.

Back in the lifetime of that early man, buried in his hollow log, the Epping Forest ridge was very different to how it is now, the pollen record indicating that the dominant species of tree was the small-leafed lime. In 1722, Daniel Defoe wrote in *Tour Through the Eastern Counties* that 'probably the Forest of Epping has been a wild forest ever since this island was inhabited, and may show us, in some parts of it, where enclosures and tillage have not broken in upon it, what the general face of this island was before the Romans landed in Britain'. Without the benefit of pollen records and vast archives of documents, Defoe couldn't have known he was wrong. Perhaps for a moment this was wildwood, that traditional image we have of a land covered by trees in a primeval innocence, 'uncorrupted' by human hands; but if so it was a short one.

It's a common misconception that 'ancient woodland' means an area that has been untouched by people. That's never the case. Every acre of an ancient woodland like Epping Forest would once have been part of an intensively managed landscape, defined by cycles of coppicing and pollarding, providing grazing for livestock and game. In Epping Forest, human interference caused the small-leafed lime, the species that once covered over 90 per cent of the land, to be replaced by the beech, hornbeam and oak we know today. Over the centuries the coexistence of humans, animals and trees created a complex and diverse ecosystem.

Ever since the Norman Conquest, and probably

before, the Epping Forest landscape existed in a delicate balance of ecological and human power. Forest,
in fact, does not mean 'a wooded place with trees' at
all, but refers to the Forest Laws that applied to the
land. The Royal Forest of Essex covered a huge area, of
which the woodlands of Epping and Hainault were just
a constituent part. (Exactly when Epping became part
of this royal forest is up for debate, but at some point,
possibly during the reign of Henry I, the Forest Laws
were applied over the area.) Deer were hunted by the
monarch and his noblemen, some taken for feasts back
in the city palaces, others given to favourites of the king
in order that they might start their own hunting parks.
England's Forest Laws were part of what gave the mon-
archy its quasi-mystical status: the king as divine ruler
with mastery over both the human and natural world.

Yet the forest was almost swept away. The British
Museum displays an 1829 Cruikshank cartoon with
the title, 'London going out of town – or – the march
of bricks and mortar!', depicting the invasion of the
countryside surrounding London by an army of building
materials. It's a pictorial version of William Morris'
description of homes for Londoners as 'hideous brick
encampments'. The dome of St Paul's is dimly visible
through thick smoke that drifts north from the massed
ranks of terraces called New Street. Chimney pots with
hods for heads and pickaxe legs march forth brandishing banners and masonry trowels. An advance guard of
their number stands over a prostrate tree, saw in hand.
A blasted trunk behind puns in its moment of demise,
'Oh! I'm mortarly wounded!' In the distance a punning

general of the arboreal forces utters a pained cry: 'Our fences I fear will be found to be no defence against these barbarians, who threaten to enclose and destroy us in all <u>manor</u> of ways.'

During the nineteenth century the landowners of south-west Essex started to enclose the forest land with the aim of turning it to agricultural use or for building as the invasion of London, aided by the growth of the railways, crept up the Lea and Roding Valleys towards it. The iron road reached Loughton in 1856, Epping in 1865 and Chingford in 1873. The Royal Forest of Hainault, on the other side of the Roding Valley from Epping, was disafforested, meaning that the old laws no longer applied. Nearly 3,000 acres were felled in just six weeks in 1851.

The violence and speed of the destruction of Hainault Forest prompted people to act to save the woodland across the Roding. Enclosure fences were broken down. Correspondence was taken up in the London newspapers. The matter was raised in Parliament, and an inquiry set up. Matters came to a head when, in 1864, the Lord of the Manor of Loughton, Revd Maitland, enclosed 1,300 acres to prevent commoners from pollarding the trees. Tradition had it that the right to do so was preserved on the condition that on 11 November each year the commoners held a lopping ceremony up in the forest. On that night in 1865 Thomas Willingale and his family broke down the fences round Staples Hill, the high part of the forest a five-minute walk from Granny's front door, and climbed up towards the trees to exercise their ancient forest right. Illustrations from the time show gnarled old trunks entirely out of scale, dwarfing the surrounding people and lit by fire and moon, with men brandishing curved blades and the women collecting piles of wood.

The Willingales were prosecuted, but supporters rallied round to their cause. Widely credited as being the first conservation movement in Britain, a 'million-pence campaign' raised funds to support the desperately poor family and pay for the legal process in defence of their right to lop. It was accompanied by virulent letter-writing to the press, with bad-tempered correspondence published under headings such as 'Madness Extraordinary'.

The coalition to save Epping Forest crossed the class divides of the time, encompassing commoners, as represented by the Willingales, local aristocrats like Lord Buxton, the media and eventually the Corporation of London, who'd been persuaded of the benefit of the forest as a place of recreation for their subjects. Crucially, thanks to a sanitation crisis down in the Square Mile, they were in a position to help. By the middle of the nineteenth century the churchyards of London were overflowing, with bodies buried on top of each other in tiny graveyards encroached upon by the fast-growing city. The ooze from the putrefying remains was threatening to pollute the water supply. The Corporation of London's solution was to purchase an area of land for a new cemetery, then going cheap out to the east of the city. Thanks to the profligacy of MP, philanderer and rake William Pole-Tylney-Long-Wellesley, nephew of the Duke of Wellington, a few thousand acres of Aldesbrook

Farm were up for sale. It was all that remained of the once great Wanstead Park Estate, its fortune frittered away by Wellesley's dissolute lifestyle. Upon his death in July 1857 while eating a boiled egg, *The Morning Chronicle*'s obituary described him thus: 'A spendthrift, a profligate, and a gambler in his youth, he became a debauchee in his manhood . . . redeemed by no single virtue, adorned by no single grace, his life has gone out without even a single flicker of repentance.' Yet had it not been for Wellesley's nefarious activities and his descendants' desperate need to raise some cash by selling Aldesbrook Farm to the Corporation of London for their cemetery, the forest as we know it today might not have been saved.

By owning the farm, the Corporation of London technically acquired commoners' rights of grazing over the entire forest land, from the fringes of the capital's sprawl to the south up into the Essex countryside past Epping in the north. They argued in the courts that the enclosure of Epping Forest was against the ancient Forest Laws. After a protracted legal case and further protests, on 8 August 1878 Disraeli's government passed the Epping Forest Act, ending its status as a royal forest with 'An Act for the Disafforestation of Epping Forest and the preservation and management of the unenclosed parts thereof as an Open Space for the recreation and enjoyment of the public; and for other purposes'.

The Act gave the Corporation legal control over the forest, which was to be maintained by a group of Conservators. The forest itself was purchased from the local landowners with money from the Metage Tax on coal and grain entering London. The ordinary people whose privations had done so much to save the forest were bought off rather cheaply. The right to lop was extinguished by the Act, £6,000 being paid by the Corporation to the people of Loughton to build Lopping Hall, a public meeting house halfway between what is now the Central Line tube station and the edge of the forest.

The forest had sustained the poor who lived around it. Their actions, and the bodies of the capital's dead, saved the forest in a reciprocal relationship of balance and renewal. In later years Thomas Willingale was commemorated by that blue plaque on the wall of the churchyard where he's buried, and a street and a school were named after him.

After a love affair ends, our need for comfort can send us back to our blood family just as much as it does into the beds of strangers, and when Alice and I broke up I spent hours on the phone to Mum. As I droned on about my feelings of regret and explained delusional theories of how I could and should have done things differently, her calm words of solace and encouragement took me back to the childlike state when I would be ill or unable to sleep and she would come and sit beside me on my bed, place her hands on my head and pray. Sometimes she would speak in tongues, whispering words in a language that I didn't understand but that she had brought to me from God. I wished I could return to that place of peace, but increasingly it seemed impossible.

I'd found Edie's funeral and Ian's death deeply affecting, perhaps surprisingly given we weren't close. That evening I lay on the grotty mattress I'd carried with me from Tower Gardens to yet another room that wasn't my own, this time in a musty attic, and stared up at the orange square of the Velux window. Mind whirring, I was all too conscious that Edie's death meant she was the last of her generation that I would know. My parents were next in line.

After a lifetime in the service of others, Dad had just retired and, with the awful timing of a carriage clock from God, received some troubling results after a test for prostate cancer. Sleep was banished by my dread of the terrible absence that must inevitably come to all sons and daughters. The police helicopter thundered overhead from its base on the other side of the forest at Lippets Hill. I imagined it flying over the black treetops surrounding the High Beach graveyard and the snake of the forest through the lights of London to the huge cemetery at its foot. As a light rain started to rattle the window above my head I fell into fitful sleep.

7

Chemistry Lessons

Granny's death closed off my childhood path into Epping Forest. There would be no more trips to her living room, clock ticking loudly while Steve Davis played snooker on the telly, where I'd sit making swirling patterns of biro ink on paper with a Spirograph. At the end of our visits, as Dad drove us towards the motorway and home I'd see the same intricate curves I'd drawn reflected in the trees as the headlamps picked out crackling circles of stark brightness against the pitchy depths beyond. It was as if the wood had become electricity and light, sparks glimpsed for a moment and then gone.

My experience of the forest then was closely linked with my parents and their love of God and nature, my child's eyes seeing it only in a sentimental, woodcut picture-postcard way. That reflected much of my life, back then. I'd been incredibly lucky to have a childhood free – unlike those of so many of my friends – of the trauma of divorce and parental discord. It's from within that privileged comfort zone that you're able to see the land outside the city as a place of respite.

My favourite things were simple – visiting relatives who lived out in the countryside with gardens in which to build camps with my cousins. I was obsessed with *Swallows and Amazons*, Rosemary Sutcliffe's *The Eagle of the Ninth*, steam trains chuntering along rural branch lines, tales of derring-do on the high seas. I'd run home from church every Sunday to watch *Countryfile* before lunch.

We had very little money, and never went on holidays abroad. Nevertheless, we were lucky in that Dad's work meant that people would often offer us places to stay during the school holidays, usually out in the countryside. Away from school and our daily routine, I felt a peace during those times that I haven't felt since. Every evening I'd write up the day's activities, drawing pictures of what we'd seen and sticking in leaflets – I loved a holiday leaflet – imagining I was writing some new *Shell Guide to Britain*.

I absorbed the British landscape as we drove around in the family car, amid a cocktail of aromas dominated by the sick bucket, a thick margarine container that smelled strongly of plastic, vomit and bleach. On those journeys my eyes would be glued to the car window, and to a soundtrack of praise songs and hymns, Vaughan Williams' 'The Lark Ascending' and Enya's 'Watermark' I would crane my neck searching for kestrels hovering over the motorway verges, or for a glimpse of distant hills. Once we hit a blackbird, and I was quietly devastated for days. Though I might for a while have seen that family car as a killing machine, it was the place where our family congregated, away from the rest of the world.

Those holidays represented everything Mum and Dad did to make sacrifices for us. They would indulge my sisters and me with fancy food like Lyons ginger cake or mini variety boxes of Kellogg's for the duration we were away, saving up so we could go on a steam train or visit a zoo. I would always be devastated when we had to return home, and one year I collected together the pennies from my savings tin and left them in an envelope in my parents' bedroom, along with a letter saying how much I loved them and how I wanted them to have the money to help pay for our holiday. Mum wrote back, saying they loved me too, but to keep the money and perhaps put half in the Methodist charity box.

After Alice and I broke up I was desperate to find a way back to how I felt during those happy childhood years, to access the simplicity of a time when my anxieties were limited to whether there'd still be Frosties among the Kellogg's boxes in the morning; or the time when, on holiday in Tenby, I heard a coastguard rocket explode, and ran faster than I ever had before in the hope of seeing the lifeboat slide down its ramp into the sea.

After Edie's funeral I spent a weekend up in Norfolk in a small house overlooking a graveyard where we'd had many happy summers when I was a child. The wall round Chapel Cottage Knapton only came up to my thigh, but it once marked the boundary of a deep canyon down which I could sail ships or, on summer days, marshal and annihilate armies of ants on the hot red tiles. The house smelled the same as it did back then, a comforting mixture of chimney tar and rattan furniture, but I kept banging my head on the door-frames. One afternoon I went to the vast beach we'd always visited and saw the same 'No Fouling' sign with a cartoon dog and a pile of shit that I'd always found so funny as a kid. The North Sea that chewed the beach where I would fish or build sandcastles was still the same grey as it always had been, but now it seemed to belong to a boy from another world. These places of fond memory no longer provided the joyous escapism they had given me as a child.

St Albans, where we lived, was dull compared to the rural England I loved to watch rushing past out of the car window or the wildernesses of my imagination. There was the lake down past the cathedral that stank of algae. Fish swam along what remained of the River Ver, its level low from over-extraction, with great wounds in their sides made by the herons to which they were prey but from whom they could no longer hide. I loved to stand and look at the fragments of wall that once surrounded the Roman city of Verulamium, burned by Boudica short-ly before she supposedly met her death in Epping Forest. I dreamed of the wildness that I was convinced must have existed outside those walls, so far removed from the sensible cars and identikit homes of the modern town. I imagined myself naked and painted in woad, skulking through the great forest. I fetishised the ancient, careful-ly carrying home a Roman tile from a flowerbed in the ruins, and held my breath underneath the giant yew that grew next to the cathedral, for someone had told me that its roots sucked out the souls of the damned and dead, and to be wary of breathing them in.

Yet just as tree hormones cause their leaves to fall in autumn, everything we hold dear can be swept away by our teenage years. Masculinity had hitherto been represented by the love I received from my dad. I grew up being told that I was a chip off the old block. People confused our voices on the telephone and told me that we had the same tendency to strong opinions and humour. When you grow up as the son of a preacher man you're permanently on show, under the scrutiny of the church congregation. It also marks you out at school as being a bit weird. Nobody dared trick or treat our house on Halloween because Dad would answer the door and use the opportunity to deliver a warning about the occult energies behind the American commercial fripperies with such gravitas that we never got tricked. I'd sit at the top of the stairs listening to him speak to the fancy-dress witches and ghouls, feeling quietly proud. Friends would come round and say in advance they were scared of meeting my parents, as if grace before tea might double up as a sermon promise of hellfire and damnation. I was proud of that too, and the inevitable moment when my friends would realise that he and my mum didn't in fact call down thunderbolts with the Angel Delight. In Dad was reflected a benevolent father God and the teachings of Jesus. At my all-male comprehensive school, my vision of what it was to be male was to take a terrible blow.

When boys hit the age of eleven or twelve and are

forced into single-gender mass companionship, a grim energy can be unleashed as pituitary glands begin the work of puberty. Almost overnight my classmates metamorphosed into grunting beasts who were no longer interested in any of the same things as I was. Everyone became obsessed by sport and their physical prowess. I hadn't learned to walk until I was nearly three, and a clodhopping clumsiness had persisted ever since. I was dire at any kind of physical exercise, treating approaching balls (be they rugby, football, basket or cricket) as if they were grenades to be avoided at all costs, running round the hurdles rather than risking the inevitable cracked ankle in athletics, and dreading the afternoons of rugby that would seem to bring the ever-present air of violence to an intense simmer among my peers. The night before PE I would be consumed with dread. I would sit on the stairs at home crying, watching the hands of the clock tick round so I could imprint them in my mind and then replay the passage of time in my safe, family cocoon the next day when I was out on the cold and bullying rugby field. Mum would pray with me and do her best to make my dread of the PE teachers – in my imagination vicious, cruel tyrants – go away. God never answered my own prayers for snow or a storm, a mad ploughman or a carpet-bombing raid by American B-52s that would render the sports field unusable.

I resented how our level of interest in and ability at sport had become the prime decider in the male hierarchy, turning boys into herds of boastful idiocy. I had been so good at being a boy but had no idea how to become a young man. I desperately didn't want to. I had nothing in common with most of those weird creatures and my confidence vanished, almost overnight. Their masculinity was reflected in their changing bodies which at once attracted and repelled me as I turned on my own, conflicted by my increasing discomfort at the hormonal physicality of my gender. I loathed my gangly form, the parts of myself that were refusing to grow hair, and I clutched my arms tight round me in my light-blue PE vest. I looked at the other boys proudly talking about how often they shaved, or standing, arms raised, earnestly discussing their 'personal bests' in athletics with the same tone in which they'd brag about touching tits or fingering girls.

Sport did have one compensation. From a young age I'd felt an attraction to other boys. At first it was curiously detached, in that typically pre-pubescent way. I experienced strange new tingling emotions when I imagined rescuing both girls and boys from the clutches of the pirates or Nazis that I had read about in books. It became something else entirely with the anxious muddle of nascent sexuality. At twelve, I developed a deep crush on a boy in my year who was as smart with words as he was good at basketball, a sport I hated. Still, it became more bearable when I could lurk around the edges of the court, avoiding the action but watching his long, brown arms and calf muscles stretching for a point or a pass.

Showers after sports were compulsory, and we were made by the teachers to leave our towels on the hook. As the years went on and potent hormones surged through me, this was both an agony and a luxury as

I'd sprint in and out of the shower, desperately trying to look and not look at the same time. 'Ugh! Ugh! he's got a boner!' someone shouted, and I quickly pulled on my pants and trousers, terrified someone had seen me. But they hadn't. It was someone else, and a few days later graffiti appeared on a garage door near the school: 'Peter Kent is so bent – Peter Pecker = boner.'

Accompanying the Tippex text was a typically juvenile drawing of a cock and balls, complete with spiky pubes and two-directional arrows to indicate tumescence. I had a pretty good idea who'd written it, a classmate whom I was sure I'd also spotted with eyes a-wander in the shower after PE. I'd looked at him too, his skinny body tanned after the school holidays but with a white bum where his trunks had been that highlighted the big dick I once saw stiffening as he hurriedly bunched a towel in front of him to hide it. My crush quickly transferred to him.

Every day at the end of school I hoped that he'd be at the gates, so we might go home the same way. After-noon after afternoon we'd walk the quiet streets, me almost dizzy with lust and panic as I tried to summon the courage to turn the conversation away from com-plaining about teachers and the day we'd just had. The graffiti gave me the opportunity. I asked if he had written it and he confessed that he had. He paused before explaining, 'He said it was an accident, and everyone believed him didn't they because he's one of the sports ones?' He admitted he felt a bit bad for saying what he did about Peter on the garage door, and then I said something that I wasn't expecting to say, that made me breathe fast and deep and the suburban street fade away as I took the leap: 'But it's quite nice, *looking*, isn't it,' I started nervously, 'Don't you look too?' He said he did. He said he went to M&S and looked at the men's underwear and went home and wanked as he thought about the models. Hardly daring to believe that it was true, I muttered, terrified, 'Would you do something with another boy and pretend it was a girl?' He stopped. 'Yes,' he said, 'but I wouldn't pretend it was a girl.' The rest of the walk before I turned off towards my house passed in awkward silence.

I didn't see him again for a whole, agonising, pent-up week, until we were sat next to each other in Chemistry class. The register had barely been taken before I pushed my leg against his and was met with an instant, firm response. If the teacher had asked me a question then I'd have struggled to reply with my name – a beautiful, dizzying rush took hold, unlike anything I'd ever known. I let my hand fall beneath the desk and gently brushed my knuckles against him. His hand vanished from the textbook, took mine and moved it slowly up the rough material of his trousers. I nearly gasped as he lifted my fingertips onto the warm skin of his hard cock, which he'd discreetly slipped out of his flies, and closed my hand round it. I'd not yet drunk alcohol, or smoked a cigarette, or done anything much that might put me in an altered state of mind, but this certainly did, my hand on another boy's erection in the middle of a lesson. The room was silent. We'd been told to read. My eyes flickered around. Everyone was absorbed in their books, the teacher in some marking. We were safe, as safe as could be. Trying not to let my arm move so as to be seen above the desk, I started to gently move my hand up and down. I felt him freeze as I pulled his cock further out of his trousers. The chemical equations on the page in front of me danced their way out of the periodic table, my heart was racing and it was only a matter of seconds before he came, all over my hand and up his light-grey school jumper. At that moment, the door swung open and the deputy headmaster walked into the room. When a senior teacher entered we had to stand up. Somehow, nobody spotted his undone flies, the wet marks on his chest, the soaked tissue clasped in my hand. That day in Chemistry I learned a valuable lesson – that getting away with things is sometimes easier than you might think.

Back in the early 1990s, sex education in schools was woeful for heterosexuals, let alone for gays, lesbians and especially those somewhere in the middle. We were shown diagrams of the reproductive organs and lectured about contraception. There was the constant implication that we, as boys, were always wanting sex whereas women would have to be, as wrong as it now sounds, persuaded into it. The girls in the other single-sex state school on the far side of town were the vestal virgins. Sex was never talked about in terms of pleasure. It was a reductive education and as hard to deal with as the growing discomfort of knowing that the Bible on my bedside table at home told me that sex, unless sanctified by marriage and between a man and a woman, was a mortal sin.

This was the time of Section 28, the Tory law that forbade the 'promotion' of homosexuality in schools. I never heard the word 'gay' or 'homosexual' uttered from the mouth of a teacher, let alone any nuanced teaching on the complexity of desire. My school had over 900 pupils, yet in my seven years there I never knew of one out gay or bisexual boy, only the bullying that was directed at anyone vaguely suspected of being a 'poof'. I was lucky that I only got picked on for being a bit of a swot and terrible at sport, and gradually learned to build up a defence of humour and by forging alliances with some of the tougher kids who didn't fit in. I knew, though, that if I got caught with my hand round Tippex Boy's cock, we'd be instantly branded 'benders', 'shirt lifters' or one of the other charming terms boys and men use to hide their fear of their own sexuality. That human instinct for binary comfort means that there's no possibility, or at least there wasn't then, that a sexual act didn't push you into one camp or the other – one touch of a cock and that was it, you were a pariah who would no doubt have been punished by the school authorities nearly as severely as your peers. A friend recently sent me a news report about how my school had been deemed 'inadequate' in a 2017 Ofsted inspection, in part because 'pupils report that they do not feel safe in the school and bullying is commonplace. Pupils often make derogatory and homophobic comments to each other and about teachers'. It was startling to read. If this was the case in the supposedly more progressive present, then my memory might even have suppressed how terrible it was a quarter of a century ago.

There were no media, cultural or educational voices to offer comfort or wisdom on what it might mean to be attracted to both men and women. Aside from deep inside my own most secret thoughts, the first time I was even aware of the wider concept of bisexuality was via an AIDS warning poster. Grimly monochrome, it showed a photograph of two clasped male hands, one with a wedding ring and one without. The poster asked, 'Do You Know Who He Is Having an Affair With?' Like most government-directed campaigns of the time, it fed into the dangerous and homophobic stereotype of HIV as a gay disease spread by feckless promiscuity. But it also marked out bisexual men as equal, or per-haps even worse, villains, transmitting the virus into the heterosexual norm and rejecting the binary constructs of sexuality that society adhered to back then.

I was too young and sheltered to have discovered David Bowie or any of the few bisexual role models who by the early 1990s were in the public eye and might have helped me see my sexual orientation as normal, nothing to be ashamed of. I'd loved *Queen's Greatest Hits*, one of the few pieces of vinyl remaining from the old collection my dad had to sell to pay his way through college. Just as I started to fall in love with the pomp and drama of the music, Freddie Mercury revealed he had AIDS, and died the following day. In the conser-vative middle England of the 1990s, the epitaph of his sexuality was a dozen tasteless playground jokes and hyperbolic headlines about disease. I worried that this might be how I was going to end up. Were all of us who wanted to have sex with men and women doomed to die of AIDS?

The high-speed rail link from St Albans to London and the financial boom of the 1980s had turned it into a commuter town, with skyrocketing house prices to match. It also sucked the life out of the place and, like most of the towns around the capital, St Albans had very little going for it anyway. It was middle-class and superficially successful, but it had no soul. Unlike in the industrial North or the agelessness of the countryside, there's nothing about these wealthy satellite towns to pin an identity on. Even the suburbs have a strange, seedy drama compared to their quiet banality. I would deliver papers up crazy-paved driveways and run from the German shepherds and labradors that came snarling through back doors. It was a deeply conservative town where the kids from school would go on foreign holidays in the summer and ski in the winter and were bought expensive trainers, posh bikes and computer games consoles. I didn't really want any of these things, but it was discomforting being marked out at the end of the holidays as someone who hadn't been abroad, and who had come to school in a new uniform umpteen sizes too big so I'd grow into it.

A rejection of perceived childlike things is part of the teenage experience, and nobody else outwardly shared my passion for the natural world. The other boys would come back at the start of each term to argue about their beloved football teams, talk about girls they'd met on holiday or films I wasn't allowed to watch. They'd spend every breaktime roughly kicking a ball around the gravelly playground while I snuck off to hide in the library to read books about hills and ships. Mostly, school had been something to be endured, dull compared to the magic I found in the maps of dreamlands that I drew. But now that started to change. I had wanted the places I drew to save me, dreaming on the PE field of the wide-open moors of my Yorkshire childhood. But of course they couldn't. It was around the time of those below-desk fumblings during Chemistry class that music became a new obsession into which I could pour my doubts, insecurities and hidden sexuality. It offered the possibility of metamorphosing into a new me, of accessing new, adult worlds. Wild places were relegated to memory.

The few overgrown patches of woodland and scrub that in places penetrated the town may have lost their childhood magic, but they also became powerful sources of titillation. Back in those pre-internet days the prospect of seeing a photograph of a naked adult was desperately yearned for. Aside from poring over the underwear section of the Kay's mail-order catalogue, the best way to satisfy eyes and arm was by scouring the bushes along any patch of waste ground or town woodland. Here, soggy and lurking in the undergrowth, were the sacred scrolls for the teenage boy – *Club* magazine, *Razzle*, the much rarer beefcakes and cocks of *Playgirl* and lesser testaments like the *Sunday Sport*. Sometimes, cruelly, nature would have got there first and turned the paper so frail that tits would disintegrate upon touch. Once I found a sacred ark – a sports holdall full of copies of *Club International* – and told someone about it. They got suspended for selling them in the playground.

The same pure, intense rush I felt playing with my friend in Chemistry lessons accompanied the discovery of a grot mag in the bushes, far more exciting I realise now than a first drink or cigarette. Small-town 1990s teenagers combed the land as effectively as forensics after a lost child. We didn't learn the names of plants or look up to see the birds that sang above us, but instead turned up the jetsam of middle England's libido in our frantic hunt – condoms, underwear, photographs of a former lover, boobs out and torn in half.

That impulse drove a generation to investigate arthouse cinema via the warnings of nudity in the *Radio Times*. That was how I started to discover the radicalism of queer culture, assisted by my love of the sexually ambiguous, blouse-wearing guitar pop band Suede. They had led me to the work of Derek Jarman, and when he died of AIDS in 1994 I stayed up late to watch *Edward II* and *Caravaggio*, nervous on the sofa with finger on the channel-hop button as the beautiful naked body of the hero of *Sebastiane* was tied to a tree and shot full of arrows. My teenage viewings of those films were charged by sexual discovery and a curiosity about art beyond the little that was taught at school. With his casts of lithe young men whose lack of formal acting training made their performances all the more naturalistically erotic, Jarman opened up a new possibility for me – homosexuality weaponised into queerness in art, in politics and as rebellion. I could not find out much about Jarman beyond those infrequent screenings and a couple of newspaper reports following his death. He became something of a mythic figure in my imagination, an alchemist who used his genius behind the camera to turn the moral opprobrium of society, the dirt of shame, into a seething power; a counter-attack. I loved how he existed in such opposition to the staid conformity of St Albans, like the music of Suede, my favourite band.

Their songs spoke of a gothic London, a city of the night with androgynous beings flitting from taxi to bed. London replaced the childhood forests and hills in my waking fantasies of escape. It seemed glamorous, seductive and strange, the other side of this city just twenty minutes away on a train. I joined the Suede fan club and went to the capital to see them play live at the Town and Country Club, queueing early and watching the band alone, lost in lust as I danced surrounded by the beautiful, androgynous fellow fan-club members with their cheekbones and straight hair and sass. I was far too shy to risk speaking to anyone.

As my head filled with music and sex, the power that the natural world had over me started to fade. Now that my granny was no longer with us I had little reason or opportunity to visit Epping Forest, and anyway my parents had moved to another town even further away from the woods I'd loved as a child.

My detachment from naive ideas of the countryside as a place of sylvan respite and the romantic pastoral versus an embrace of the urban was rather wonderfully reflected in Bruce Robinson's frequently homoerotic *Withnail and I*. When I first saw it as a teenager it instantly became my favourite film. Two effete resting actors but very active alcoholics attempt to take the traditional rural remedy, as the 'I' character puts it: 'We are indeed drifting into the arena of the unwell. Making an enemy of our own future. What we need is harmony. Fresh air. Stuff like that.' It doesn't go as planned. The rural retreat is essentially a ruin, the landscape inhospitable – 'There's nothing out there but a fucking hurricane' – and uncanny – 'Those are the kind of windows faces look in at,' and the locals are unfriendly. Desperate for food and wood for the fire, I visits a local farm, trying to win over a rugged farmer's wife by reassuring her that 'We're not from London, you know.' 'I don't care where you come from,' she snaps back, slamming the door in his face. My imagination had already moved to that London. I wanted to breathe its air and let it poison me.

I loved my parents too much to commit the obvious teenage acts of rebellion – sullen insolence, drinking enough in a park to chuck it all up again over the family car. Perhaps that might have been a better outlet given what was to happen, but I was desperate not to upset them. The only overt act of transgression I'd committed was a brief spell running the Tory campaign at a school mock election in 1992 and putting up a picture of the St Albans MP, Peter Lilley, in my bedroom window. After then, everything I did that went against their beliefs was quiet, private, secret, unknown to anyone except myself.

But in a way I liked my hidden inner life. I knew that it marked me out as different from the male heterosexual norms that I found so oppressive at school. It may be part of growing up for teenagers to act out against the adult world, but I found the overtly masculine way in which my peers did it exclusionary and deeply off-putting. Their maleness, peacocked through their constant play-fighting and sporting prowess, the cruel persecution and the banter, revolted me. Instead, my taboo sexuality fuelled my own personal rebellion against the endless tirade of homophobic insults that flew around the school corridors. It was my secret challenge to the vulgar mundanity of a Home Counties commuter town that felt utterly devoid of culture, where as we got (just about) old enough to start going to pubs I and my friends frequently had to run from a kicking. I wore women's blouses, dyed my hair red, a provocation to those boys from school and the men on the street I saw as brutish, lager-swilling pigs. Yet that private, grey area of sex that nobody knew of except my friend was a lonely space. I might have been laughed at on the rugby field when a hurtling ball cracked against my fingers and yet again span off in some random direction across the mud, but later, at home, hands down my trousers as I replayed the captured memory of my favourites naked in the shower, I felt as if I was having my revenge.

There was no rosy coming-of-age story of sexual awakening, a blossoming love between two young men. Just the urgent, mutual lust that accompanies the need for convenience and nothing more. It was at the time when my hormones had started to trace the contours of my own map of sexual desire, but what might have been a fairly innocent release for it all was cut off. Tippex Boy decided his exploration of bisexuality was just a phase and, during one Chemistry lesson later that term, pushed my hand away. I was left to compose earnest letters and mix tapes for the few girls I knew from the church youth group, trying to hide my darting eyes in the shower after PE. I felt that typical teenage loneliness often dealt with by vanishing into books and music and dreaming of getting away from it all, equally matched by endless hours of fantasy. I had learned the art of concealment, from my family, from God, from my peers. With no outward means to express these conflicts and feelings, my mind started to turn against itself. Under the desk in Chem Lab II part of me had been awakened, but with no way of continuing to satisfy that elemental desire, my instinct started to spiral out of control. I did not realise that I had become bait.

8

The Garden

I discovered Greensted Church, the oldest wooden building in Europe, via a Pathé newsreel and a Google search, and found it via a coughing bus to Chipping Ongar Sainsbury's, slightly delayed thanks to a joyrider smash on the mean streets of North Weald. At the start of the public footpath to the church a decapitated pigeon was being eaten by frantic wasps. A row of solitary oaks continued across flat, open fields, marking the line of a long-vanished hedgerow. As I walked from tree to tree I tried to imagine the ancient landscape through which the early pilgrims had trod, full of zeal in their mission to create a place of worship in the heart of the woods. Analysis of the vertical oak planks, or staves, of Greensted Church's wall, curved on the outside and adzed flat in the interior, suggests that the trees were felled nearly 1,000 years ago and came from an area of continuous forest rather than pasture or hedgerow. There's evidence too of a far older wooden structure on the site, perhaps the chapel in which the martyred body of the Saxon King Edmund was said to have rested in 1013.

To the right over a low hedge a giant swan made me jump – but it was just a pedalo, floating on the lake of a mansion that now housed Greensted Church's closest parishioners. I doubted they went much, Christmas and at a push Easter perhaps, and felt sad about that, as I always do when I think of religious decline – especially mine.

I've been visiting places of worship since the day I was born but hadn't been so much recently. I fell away from it all during those teenage years when the Christian teachings of sexuality had crashed awkwardly into the reality of my hidden life. Now, two decades later, I was starting to realise that everything I was searching for in my repeated visits to the forest and these dives into its history was an attempt to come to terms with what I had neglected to deal with then, thinking that if only I suppressed the conflicts they might go away.

I opened the final gate and entered the graveyard. The timbers of the church's walls were sturdy even after nearly a millennium, the tiled roof was quaint and the tower shrouded in scaffolding. Online I'd found one of those Lilliput Lane china models of the church, an idealised version of an idealised version, but the real thing didn't have any of that rustic twee. It lurked ahead of me with all the presence and power of a courtroom Bible. I wanted to find the peace of God in this ancient place just as acutely as I had been hunting for comfort in the fleeting encounters my buzzing iPhone so effortlessly provided.

The Christian faith was never forced upon me, but it was all I had ever known. Although I was teased and seen as odd for having a preacher as a dad, I was always proud of the unconventional life we led. I still have the Gideons Bible that was given to us at school, in it my name and the date, 27 November 1990, in handwriting that's clearly me trying to be reverential and neat with my new fountain pen but I can see now still displays the wobble of childhood. The red-bound book was a beautiful and sacred thing, and I was angry with the idiot boys who'd desecrated their copies with drawings of Satan or tits, or even burned them in the playground or flushed them down the loo. To me, the non-religious seemed like the weirdos, missing out on the caring, good-natured communities that had always surrounded my family. The Christian faith had offered me peace and something far more profound – the metaphysical strangeness of seeing people speaking in tongues, healing, prophecy, and the intoxicating surge of the Holy Spirit at a charismatic gathering. These were my first experiences of the intensely psychedelic and they moved me.

My mum grew up in the Brethren, an exclusive, strict Christian sect that forbade television, radio, pop music and, eventually, most interactions with non-Brethren people. Her family left in the early 1960s when the Brethren took an even more terrifying turn towards the autocratic, but still held on to many of its hard-line views on sexuality and gender. Mum was never a harsh judge, however, and these views were eclipsed by her love, her endless sacrifices for my sisters and me and her gift of reassurance via the speaking in tongues. As the child of a preacher you spend many long hours waiting to leave places while parents talk or services go on. When I was small I would lie with my head in her lap during hymns and prayers, comforted by the vibrations within her body of the sacred words and melodies she sang with such conviction and joy. I grew fast in those early teenage years and was soon taller than her. I'd rest with my elbows on her shoulders, trying to return to those days of comfort, but I was too heavy now, and too tall.

A child brought up with the enveloping love of family and the Christian faith is given a rich and detailed map to follow that will take him or her through life. Its contours are stories that don't offer an escape from the trials of existence, but do show a path through them: for every situation there is a key and a guide. The routes and danger zones are marked out with pinpoint accuracy. Look at an OS map of a forest and you'll see the woodland represented by the occasional tree on a green background. The faith I knew wasn't thin like that, but had in its cartography everything you might see along the way, down to the tiniest grain of sand. Faith was indivisible from real life. I've seen this map used by many I care for and love, but not blindly – for any sensible Christian questions it, is sometimes enraged by it, always struggles with doubts. It was with growing confusion at my developing, complicated sexuality that as a teenager I looked at the map and saw great chasms opening up, the lakes and pillars of fire, sin and death. Lot's wife turned away from the map and back to

Sodom and she became a pillar of salt. That one stuck with me.

It was this awareness that my sexuality didn't fit in with the heterosexual expectations of either my Christian faith or the boorish masculine school around me that made me start to disappear within myself. It didn't help that I had grown up with a binary mindset, believing in heaven and hell, good and evil, saint and sinner, straight and gay, city and countryside. God had made me a certain way, and yet I could feel my desires cleaving to the unnatural, the most cardinal of all sins. I was impure, corrupt. There was always talk of people who had 'gone off the rails' and I desperately didn't want to become one of them.

It didn't and doesn't help that the more extreme and judgemental voices in Christianity might consider heterosexual adultery a sin and homosexuality an abomination: to be bisexual was to carry two damnations in one. To be gay or bisexual was against nature as God intended. This view didn't always come from my immediate family, who had a relatively nuanced approach to sexuality. When a member of the church congregation was arrested for having sex with his male partner in a public place, Dad stood up for him in a disciplinary case that tried to get him removed from his position as a teacher.

Growing up in a religious family, you have three parents – mother, father and God. If you're lucky, as I was, the love from your parents is both human and filtered through the positive love of the Christian faith. Yet the God parent is a more complicated character.

Much that I read in the Bible or picked up from wider interpretations of Christianity made me feel that I could never be accepted the way I was. There was the God 'who so loved the world that he sent his only son', but bound up with him was the God who presided over a 'fallen' and sinful world of which the sins of the flesh were the greatest. I had held Tippex Boy's big and beautiful cock in my hand and loved every intoxicating minute of it, but was that not a sin? There was a song I had sung so many times as a kid: 'Jesus loves me yes I know, for the Bible tells me so'. Yet did the Bible not also tell of the terrible things that should be done to men who lay with other men? Yes, much of that was in the Old Testament, but in the Sermon on the Mount Jesus himself had said: 'If your right hand causes you to sin, cut it off and throw it away! It is much better for you to lose one of your limbs than to have your whole body go off to hell.' God knew what I had done with my hand. He had seen. I knew it from the Communion collect. *Almighty God, to whom all hearts are open, all desires known, and from whom no secrets are hidden.*

I knew Jesus loved sinners. I knew I could repent. But God had made me this way, so how could my sexuality be a sin? I was confused. It was as if a cartoon angel sat on one shoulder and a devil sat on the other, both screaming into each ear. If the thought of doing something was as bad as the act, then what choice did anyone have but to go ahead and do it anyway? And if one sin was enough for damnation, then what was the point in resisting the temptation to do it again? It's not for nothing that the Pet Shop Boys' 1987 number-one hit single 'It's a Sin' with its opening lines of 'When I look back upon my life it's always with a sense of shame' became my favourite pop song.

As much as I still believed in God, took Communion and felt the deep comfort to be found in prayer and hymn, the aggression of many practitioners of the Christian faith burned me. Ideas about conversion therapy, that sexuality can be prayed or punished away, are never as far from the Christian mainstream as you might think. As a toddler I used to look at the stern religious tracts my mum's father used to send the family while I sat on the potty. I was fascinated by the words, even when I held the pamphlets upside down. Perhaps I had somehow absorbed the teachings by cosmic osmosis and was now punishing myself.

I had constant nightmares about being followed and put on trial by shadowy figures who would condemn me to execution and the void. During those night-time visions I would try to say the name of Jesus to save me, but the cry would remain stuck in my choking throat. When I closed my book and switched off the light I would pray for a good night's sleep with no bad dreams – the words even today have retained the familiarity of a mantra – but still the terrors would come.

My parents had brought me up with nothing but love. I had absolute respect for them. Alienated by the brute masculinity that I encountered at school, it was to them that I turned for support. Yet at the heart of their love was God, whose love didn't seem quite so unconditional as before, and it became a source of pain. We were and are still a close family, yet I was aware that my under-the-desk rummages and fascination with the radicalism of the queer culture I was finding in Jarman's films or Suede's music was at absolute odds with the Christian faith at the core of our family life.

The result was turmoil and entanglement, confusion and doubt and the certain naivety that such a sheltered upbringing can cause. One afternoon I stayed out a little later than I had promised and felt consumed by guilt that, underage, I'd watched a 15-rated film. And that was without the under-desk experimentation.

It was an absolute agony to think that my sexual identity was seen by millions who had grown up with the same hymns and Bible readings as I had as an abomination to be punished by an eternity in hell. I thought I had it easy compared to a gay teenager, whose entire existence would come crashing up against the pressures of religion and its views on sin, but my bisexuality was confusing even without this choking feeling of being judged.

The turmoil didn't just come from faith, however. With no education or role models, I struggled to understand what my bisexual identity was. Was it half and half, as if I had heterosexual and homosexual sides of the self as separate modes into which I might dip or veer between? The truth is more complex, of course, because sexuality is part of every single cell, every thought, desire and belief. But I couldn't possibly have understood that as a child.

Over time, I began to believe it'd be easier for me to compartmentalise, to shut away and hide the 'gay' self and let the 'straight' one dominate: to repress the 'side' of myself that was causing such discomfort. I longed to be one or the other, not realising that by this foolish attempt to split myself in two I was inadvertently setting myself up for a conflicted future. I once blamed my bisexuality alone for this, believing that it wasn't possible for the heterosexual majority or homosexual minority to understand the complexity of my desires, that being attracted to both genders would inevitably poison any relationship with one or the other sex. As a teenager and even beyond I tried to fight this elusive, eddying desire, a sexual landscape that decided which way I was going to turn, rather than allowing me a clear passage through myself. All the while I felt watched by the baleful eye of God which, however loving, still carried the judgement of sin.

It wasn't as if the queer world offered much support. Bisexuals are perceived to be a threat to heteronormative culture, louche, priapic and oversexed, greedy males for whom any hole's a goal. Yet from the other side, from our gay brothers and sisters, the animosity is often even worse. I can understand that to many gay men, who have struggled with familial non-acceptance and the weary, daily reality of homophobia, a bisexual man seems to be having his cock and eating it, enjoying the freedoms afforded the heterosexual community while hiding away from the risks and prejudices. But bisexuals have been denied the radical power of their queerness precisely because it is the ultimate rejection of binaries, be they heteronormative, moral, societal, religious, familial or increasingly even homonormative. We are pushed underground with an all too frequent scorn, a patronising insistence that we're just going through a phase before finally coming out as 'properly' homosexual. While it was flattering to once be told that 'you wouldn't be able to suck a cock like that if you weren't gay', the belittling of bisexuality as mere cowardice is a cruel insult. There are further taunts: 'You'll come out when your parents are dead and you're no longer afraid' particularly hurt me, not least because it was the one that always slithered around my own sense of who I was.

However many letters might get added to what was once merely LGB and whatever the advances in the acceptance of gay men and lesbians into society – and progress there has not been as swift as some might like to make out – it doesn't feel like we're making much headway when it comes to male bisexuality. I can chalk up my years spent on gay websites and apps and so on as empirical research into the matter. Of the many hundreds of bisexual men I've spoken to in this anonymous digital hinterland, the number who were out to friends and family could be counted on one hand. Even IRL, I've rarely met a self-identifying bisexual man. Many of them have been in relationships with unknowing women. I would ask if their partner knew they were bisexual and the answer would always come back with a surprised 'Of course not, she'd kill me if she did.' To some, this might just prove prejudiced people right who claim that these men are lurking on hook-up apps and websites in search of any anonymous sex they can get. But it seems to me that it speaks more of the loneliness that is so often at the heart of their bisexuality, a lack of dialogue both with society and within relationships that might unpick the prejudice.

After I left home it didn't get any easier. I longed to live in a place that was not defined by the simplicity of masculinity alone, but had a rude awakening on my first day at university. I'd been put on the ground floor of the halls of residence, and as other people started to arrive that day it quickly became clear that this meant they were all to be men. They were mostly alright, but prone to the sort of laddish pranks that made my skin crawl. My university had an LGB society and a Christian Union, but I didn't feel welcome at either: it was as if their B was rather smaller and considered less significant than the L and the G, and I was worried about the judgement of a conservative CU. I'd have to try and find my own way through.

One night, I met a boy at the pub. We were in a big group of people talking, both of us sat on the edge, and I kept catching his eye. Outside at the end of the night, amid the rush of overexcited people saying goodbye to their new friends, the backs of his fingers brushed against my hand and I looked up, but he was already away up the concrete stairs to the bus and some awful-sounding club in town. We'd all been given our first email addresses on the then new-fangled internet and, as I had nobody else to send messages to, in the lonely weeks at the start of university I started writing to him. Obsessed as I was, it didn't take me long to start talking about Suede. I sent him their lyrics, laboriously typed out from the sleeves, and my emails gradually took on a certain hue – 'we kiss in his room to a popular tune', 'you pierce your right ear you pierce your heart oh the skinny boy's one of the girls', 'I want the style of a woman, the kiss of a man'. It worked, and he ended up responding in kind: 'I'm eighteen and I need my heroine', 'in your council home he jumped on your bones . . .'. This went on for a few days, until we met for a drink and it wasn't very long before we were stretched out on my single bed and pulling each other's clothes off. He left in a hurry in the morning, both of us afraid that the lads who lived on my corridor would see him.

Later that day I rushed to the internet room and, flushed with excitement, came out to my two female friends back home by writing to tell them I might have a boyfriend. I emailed him and said it was ace to have met someone who saw Suede in the same way as I did. But he replied confessing that he wasn't really a Suede fan at all, and had in fact been using Suede fansites (it was the early days of the internet and I didn't even know such things existed) to look up lyrics. He hoped I didn't mind. But I did mind, and decided I didn't like him very much.

Away from the cocoon of home, I still struggled to find a clear path. I knew I was attracted to both men and women and had a girlfriend for while, but it was hard for me to unpick whether I was actually a gay man, my true sexuality being repressed by an ingrained religious dogma and respect for my parents. I struggled to take pleasure in sex with men or women with the absolutist view that unless it was sanctified by marriage it was a cardinal sin. I knew that this was difficult for my parents to understand, which was why Mum and I had painful clashes over her view that homosexuality was unnatural in the eyes of God. It was so hard to reconcile these opinions with my knowledge that my sexuality had been part of me since birth, that it was ordained by a spiritual power I saw manifest in the natural world around me.

Despite all this, and unlike many who've grown up in the arms of religion, I'd never been able, let alone wanted, to scream at God or deny the possibility of energies beyond our understanding. It might have been easier if, like so many others, I had rejected the entire system of belief, but I've never been able to – for in it I still found much to hold on to.

Growing up in the Methodist tradition, the positives of the Christianity I knew were many. John Wesley, the founder of the Methodist Church, was one of the great radicals of the eighteenth century. Over the course of his life he rode over a quarter of a million miles through the United Kingdom and beyond, preaching to the working people of city, countryside and forest with a directness that they understood. Methodism had a profound impact on every community it reached, not merely promising a seat in heaven after a life of drudgery but actively working to improve the lives of people during the flicker of their time on earth. The Church went on to be instrumental in the formation of the trade union movement, the abolition of slavery and the founding of the Labour Party.

It was the Christian radicals with whom I connected, Wesley and the Ranters and Levellers, Gerrard Winstanley and his doctrines of common ownership of land; Kett's Rebellion in 1549 which, presaging the Willingales and the movement to save Epping Forest, broke down fences and disrupted enclosures as they made demands to 're-model the values of the clergy'. Religion as I understood it was always countercultural, just like the music with which I'd become obsessed. I loved the inclusiveness of Methodism, where as many as forty different nationalities might be represented in Dad's church every Sunday morning; aside from a crammed and grimly silent tube carriage in rush hour I couldn't think of many places so ethnically diverse. Nevertheless, what I had absorbed of the doctrines of sin and shame had pushed my relationship with the faith and Church into an impossible corner.

As I made my way towards Greensted that day, I thought of how place, nature and religion had almost been indivisible for me. Everywhere we'd lived was decided by God. We'd always go to church on holiday. Moreover, the closest that I'd felt to faith had always been out in the natural world – on a church weekend in Blackpool where waves forced by a huge storm gouged chunks from the promenade; in Devon's Valley of the Rocks near the Christian holiday centre of Lea Abbey; visiting an old chapel that Dad was converting into a youth hostel up in the Yorkshire Dales. It was physically present in Methodism too, Wesley having preached on the green slopes of Gwennap Pit in Cornwall. I wanted this Essex countryside, and the church that had sat within it for so many centuries, outlasting and outliving the men who defined what faith would be, to reconnect me with that intimate presence of God.

All religion is a matter of interpretation, schisms, new philosophies, ideas put forward by men that were then adopted to become orthodox. Morality is defined as much by those who came after Jesus Christ as by the teachings of the man himself. And in these endless reinterpretations and adaptations, morality too has become intertwined with place. Just as it has with sexuality, Christianity has always had a difficult relationship with the forest. Many interpretations of Genesis hold that when God created Adam in his image, it was with the purpose of having dominion over nature. But when he and Eve were tempted to eat the apple from the tree of knowledge they, and for ever after all of us, were cast out of paradise, becoming shamefully aware of our naked human forms. In our exile from the Garden of Eden is both our confusion over sexuality and gender and a separation from the natural world.

Vico, whose giants wandered the forests in bestial abandon – or free sexuality, to take a more positive interpretation – out of sight of God, states that 'The woods themselves were condemned by Moses to be burned wherever the people of God extended their conquests.' St Augustine, who turned from a dissolute life of sexual profligacy to fervent faith and the development of the doctrine of original sin, wrote of how the truth of God might best be divined from a hilltop clearing amid the woodland. Writing about his own life in *Confessions,* published in 1792, he said: 'In such a wilderness so vast, crammed with snares and dangers, behold how many of them I have lopped off and cast from my heart, as thou, O God of my salvation, hast enabled me to do' – 'wilderness' for the original text's *'immensa silva'* has been translated also as 'forest' and 'jungle'. The Christian God, then, might enable sinners to clear the forest of temptation from around themselves.

As Christianity continued to spread into Europe, the forests were seen as the preserve of the pagan, the evil and the outcasts. With a sole divine being, old beliefs in the *genius loci*, the spiritual power of sacred groves, springs or other objects in the landscape, were seen as sacrilegious and their power neutered by the construction of Christian holy places – early Christianity knew all about how to co-opt the old beliefs before destroying them. The ancient Greensted Church, with its name so referential to the woodland, might have been just such a place.

It was a warm day and I was flustered and hot, yet I felt an instant calming coolness as soon as I pushed open the door and stepped into the darkness of the nave. The ancient timbers of Greensted know no hypocrisy or bigotry, but are prayers carved from nature, as sacred as hymns. The church of the forest has no walls. These myths and histories, the hundreds of years during which this enclosed air has circulated around and through forgotten generations, have afforded Greensted its peace. Yet for all its age, it feels alive, no mere relic. I don't believe you have to have any faith to find calm in a church like this. These are communal buildings, often left unlocked for anyone to enter, and as such feel increasingly necessary in a time when so much of our public space is being sealed off from us and homogenised by the bland corporatism of modern urban development.

The wind gusted outside, the stained-glass muttering in opposition, and as I stood before the altar I experienced a flush of peace that had been refusing to come to me for months. I closed the door behind me, the wood still warm in the sunlight that mottled the grass of the churchyard into a broken watery shimmer.

9

A Whisper in the Vestry

That day I had planned to make a pilgrimage from Greensted to High Beach Church, the place that had via my granny's painting become totemic in my imagination of my family's past. But I'd been over-optimistic about my pace, and the sun had started to set beyond the distant forest, far to the west. I had to find the bus home.

A few weeks before, High Beach had become something far more significant, not just a fondly conjured destination in the heart of the forest but, in my mind, perhaps the key to decoding the family legend and my own conflicted identity. My curiosity about the family rumour that had been circulating for many years had become loaded with potential. By proving it to be true I thought I might snooker the dour moralising of those Christians by whom I always felt most judged. I felt reassured by the idea that without the breaking of the Commandment 'Thou shalt not commit adultery' some time in the distant past, I would not exist.

In a box drawn down from my dad's cousin's loft

I'd found dozens of old postcards written to a George William Turner at Manor Farm, High Beach in the late nineteenth and early twentieth century. Postcards were a cheap form of communication in the age before a widely available telephone network, used for messages as brief as those we might today send in a text. Many were signed 'Ted', dealing with plans for visits: 'My dear F & M, just a line to say I have got Saturday morning off. Hope you are both well, in haste, Ted.' Another depicted a path curving away through a rockery at the formal gardens at Kew, dated 27 February 1905: 'Dear mother, don't say I never send you a postcard, love to you both, Ted.' One more from Forest Gate reassured his parents they'd got home at 10 p.m. and 'never had long to wait at Stratford'. I knew Ted was my grandad's father, a gardener, making George my direct ancestor – in the right place, at the right time to suggest that the rumour of an illegitimate birth might be true.

I got in touch with the vicar of High Beach Church, who told me that I was welcome to come and have a look at the records of baptisms and burials stored in the vestry. She suggested I time my visit to join one of the tea and cake afternoons that the church runs every Sunday during the warmer months.

The following week at the church the vicar opened an old square safe that sat in the corner of the vestry, lurking beneath a rack of vestments. There must be thousands of those iron chests in English vestries, squat and neglected below hangers of stoles and cassocks and shelves of tatty Bibles. Inside are the records of the comings and goings of millions of otherwise undocumented lives. Methodism might have its doctrinal differences with the Church of England, but their places of worship often have a similar scent and atmosphere: an old smell of slight damp and paper, over-mashed tea and orange squash, polished wood. Just as when I hear the familiar opening chords of a favourite hymn, I feel a Proustian rush that makes me feel instantly at ease.

I stood at the back of the church, resting the leather-bound record book on a table next to that morning's order of service. The old leather spine creaked, and a musty waft rose from the paper. The early pages dealt with the now demolished original High Beach Church, which had stood somewhere out there in the forest. Faded handwriting from different vicars, some more legible than others, filled the little boxes as the nineteenth century advanced, the slow accumulation of life in this sparsely populated corner of Essex. And then, there it was. On 27 August 1854, baptism No. 152, George William Turner. Mother: Mary Ann Turner. No father. In the space where my great-great-great grandfather's occupation should have been recorded, a word had been written but then heavily scrubbed out.

A boy born who took the name of his mother. The rumour, it seemed, might be true. I had found that my family's forest story had begun with something illicit, a strange appearance of a baby with no father and just a mother in the baptismal records of a church that was no longer there. I doubted that anyone over the past century and a half had looked at this page with the excitement that I did as, with shaking hands, I pulled out my phone to take a photo of the sepia page and its careful script.

I opened a second book, the record of the burials scattered round the church in its quiet graveyard of wonky stones and towering trees. The number of each grave correlated with a churchyard plan, a life packed away into a small rectangle of ink and forest ground. I hadn't expected to see the Turners, or quite so many of them, suddenly appear under the forest soil around me. Burial No. 15 on 10 September 1885, my great-great grandmother and George's first wife, Elizabeth Rose Turner, aged thirty-three. On the next page, No. 17, their son Thomas Alfred Turner, 15 December 1885, aged eight months. Twelve years on, 9 August 1897, Percy Turner interred aged eighteen years. He might be the one who by family legend drowned, whose grave my dad visited, and after whom my grandfather was named. Into the twentieth century, Emma Rebecca Turner, George's second wife, buried in the same grave as Percy in 1924 aged eighty-six before, on 3 July 1937, George himself finally joined them.

The Turner graves are all unmarked, and as I walked out of the church the flare as my eyes adjusted to the dazzling spring afternoon was as if my ancestors had risen from their bones six feet beneath to greet me in light. I thought of my grandparents, cremated and scattered on the flowerbeds of the City of London Cemetery that had been so crucial in saving Epping Forest far down at its southern tip. I tried explaining it all to two old ladies who'd come over to see what I was doing; although they were interested, I couldn't adequately convey the great waves of emotion that were washing over me. This place that I had been coming to for years was suddenly alive with generations of my dead ancestors. We were there, through the forest from top to bottom, because deep in the past two people had committed a mortal sin. It was at once liberating and entirely daft. I couldn't think of many people who'd go to such lengths in search of such a transgression, but this tiny moment meant so much to me. The shame and guilt that I'd acquired from the oppressive elements of Christianity took a knock that day in the church, quiet but for the steamy wheezing of the tea urn in the far corner.

A PA system had been set up outside by the porch, still decorated with an arch of flowers for a wedding the day before. People sat at tables scattered around the graveyard as the vicar and a small choir led us through a few hymns, the late afternoon chill filtering through the trees and forcing brews down swiftly. Some sang along, others looked on bemused. There was a prayer of thanksgiving and hope that the church and its work in the forest might offer a place of respite from the pressing demands of London. I felt a thousand miles from the city, a century from the present day. There was nothing not to respect about this short and simple act of devotion and community taking place six feet above the bones of my ancestors. 'Thine Be the Glory', my favourite hymn and one that always sets off tears, drifted across the graves that cast shadows in the thin spring light. I mouthed along to the Lord's Prayer and felt the old rush of calm that would descend when I was ill or upset and couldn't sleep and Mum would put her hand on my head and speak in tongues.

As the tables and chairs were packed away, I took my leave through the lychgate out through the forest and towards the tube. The trees were painted a sickly hue by the last rays of the sun, not yet strong enough to offer much warmth in the late afternoon. Feeling the ghosts of these new-found ancestors at my back, I was glad to reach the open grass of Theydon Plain. Strong winds had blown the sky clear for the pale wisp of an early-rising moon, a blackthorn petal licked and pressed against the sky. It wasn't yet so dark that I couldn't see the familiar figure lumbering along, hunched and laden down with carrier bags slung across his shoulders and back. The man who lived in the forest. Its sentinel and, I felt, my friend. I shouted his name. He stopped and turned to face me. I ran towards him (I never run), calling his name again. It was only when I was a few metres away that he raised his arm in a wave and called out, 'Luke! You isn't it? Well, well, well. I thought you were a forest spirit, come to take me.'

IO

The Hanged Man

Finding the evidence that my existence was predicated on a relationship outside the morality of Victorian England and the Christian present day alike had, after those moments of joy in the churchyard, not given me quite the resolution I had hoped for. I'd got back from Greensted Church full of excitement, sending photographs of the baptismal and burial documents to the family WhatsApp group. They were interested, of course, but I couldn't convey what it was I hoped that it would mean for me. And with that, the foolishness of my endeavour started to dawn on me.

I had carried shame with me for so long that it wasn't an external pressure any longer but had settled deep inside me. No secret from generations ago would lift that weight off my back. I was foolish to have thought I was doing anything more than clutching at straws. I was still caught up in a thicket of confusion and self-doubt. I was trapped by more than God and shame, but I couldn't find a way to free myself.

The brutal full stop at the end of a long relationship always unleashes a deluge of pent-up doubts, a chaos that you must dive back into repeatedly to salvage the parts of yourself still worth hanging on to, for the re-building. That was familiar to me, but not this growing awareness that it wasn't just five years of love gone wrong that I was sifting through in these murky depths, but the thirty-one years before, that somewhere within that time was a cruel shock that still brought me down.

The intense relationship that I had got into too quickly after Alice and I broke up had flickered back into being for a moment, then ended again. There was no way I could truly connect with someone else when months on I had left more than a few old books and records at Alice's house. She was still in my dreams, smiling and close and telling me where I had gone wrong. I would dread an invitation to the pub or a gig near her place, unable to bear being in the living museum of our shared memories. Now and then we'd meet up to chat and drink, but it'd just prolong the agony of it all as I left everything that I wanted to say unsaid. When we parted I always looked back to see her for one last moment before she disappeared round the corner.

Frustrated that it was taking so long to heal, I once again sought liberation in abandon, losing evenings and days in encounters with men and women that seemed only to chip a little more of myself away. If I'd felt trapped by the constraints of a monogamous hetero-sexual relationship, then what I thought I'd wanted in its stead was proving far worse. I was starting to see that the pain I was feeling had nothing to do with bisexuality. It wasn't as if I felt any more ashamed after a threesome with an artist and his boyfriend than I did after a casual hook-up with an old female friend. The aftermath of the stripping, the biting, the tongues, the fuck performed with no intimacy was not cold because of the gaze of holy judgement. It was a look into a mirror in which I could see only an icy ghost peering back.

I was more confused than I had ever been. If I was making progress unpicking the ideas of sin that had made my sexuality so conflicting for me as a teenager, why was it causing me so much hurt? Friends seemed to look on my somewhat louche way of being with envy, and I was offering them amusing fruity anecdotes now and then. But inside, the cycle of sexual craving and consummation was causing havoc. In taking me to High Beach Church and uncovering the truth of the family rumour, the forest had given me a tool to deal with Christian guilt and shame. But I needed something more.

Throughout the long, humid month of May I tried to make the forest work for me as a place of respite and healing, in that way we're always told nature can. The Japanese have a concept called *shinrin-yoku*, or 'forest bathing', the belief that touching and smelling trees during a short woodland walk might reduce stress, lower blood pressure, and even help those who suffer from diabetes. First conceptualised in 1982, scientific studies have since set out to prove that phytoncide, essential oils released by trees, might, when inhaled by the forest bather, boost the immune system. The idea has, unsurprisingly, caught on with wellness enthusiasts and mindfulness gurus the world over, especially in the USA. It is not for me to dispute Japan's learned scientists who study forest bathing, but that spring it was as if the thick air under the leaves and the fog of what my mind had carried into the forest had condensed to drown rather than cleanse me.

The sanctity of nature extolled in the writings of the likes of Rousseau, Thoreau and the Romantic poets shapes an Enlightenment view of the forest that was at the heart of the late-nineteenth-century zeal to save it. In the early twenty-first century we see it watered down to the sentimental and twee, with photographs of forests as memes complete with a trite and 'inspirational' slogan, or 30dayswild hashtags on social media.

We tend to think of great open vistas as being edifying, capable of freeing the spirit. In the same way, we talk of 'needing space' to instil a sense of calm. But even in the daylight the murk of woodland can oppress and confuse, horizons being lost in the density of the trees. There is no space, just the intimate whirling mass that surrounds you, limbs and twigs through which your eyes cannot see. The forest becomes an organism that traps you inside it. And then, it invades you. Just look at how the human nervous system resembles the anatomy of a tree, thicker trunks spidering out to branches. I picture those structures reaching into and tangling with our nerves and veins and limbs and arteries, possessing us and dragging us back to a pre-modern state of mind. For those of us who spend our existence in the city, absorbing its stories and the lives of those around us, then this possibility becomes heightened. If in our ancient imagination the forests were home to our predators, and later were where outsiders, criminals and ne'er-do-wells were held back from the city, they have always been places of terror. Indeed, forests are in the roots of neurological responses to threat, more deeply hardwired into us than those modern anxieties that are sustained by the intravenous drip of worry that is social media.

Aside from the fantasies we are told as children or the ancient narrative of disquiet and distemper that might sit within our DNA, the city dweller knows little about why the trees look as they do, and how the paths have come to be. Into this vacuum steps fear.

I had been failing to connect with the forest during the day and acquired the stupid idea that perhaps it might be easier at night. I had always been told that danger lurked in the darkness beyond the glow of the city, but I thought the challenge might do me some good, like a cold shower, a plate of bitter greens or a Buddhist thrashing.

On a Monday evening a few weeks after that visit to High Beach Church I left work and took the train north. The grass on the fringes of Chingford Plain nearest to the station, masonic hall, Flabélos fat-removal clinic and golf clubhouse that are the final buildings of London were a velveteen ripple in the last of the light. In the shallows of Epping Forest, a group of middle-aged women in pastels circled round their instructor, all Lycra and bulges, as he encouraged them to lean and stretch with motivational yaps. Out on the landing strip for model aircraft mown into the longer grass a group of lads raced radio-controlled drones. The electrical hiss of a bright LED-covered cruciform model zipped the sky apart around my head, performing stunts against the deep-blue and silver clouds that hung over London. To the north, thick grey rain smeared over the embers of the sunset. I was caught in a pincer between a storm and the night that crept from the east. The shrill sigh of the drone receded as I waded towards the treeline through hip-high grasses, bramble patches and white spray of the hawthorn blossom as if from a beach into the waves and deepening waters of the sea.

Now that the leafy spring canopy had shivered out and closed between me and the coagulating sky, under the surface of the forest night fell before the sunset. My senses gradually started to skew as I swam into the forest, eyes struggling to accustom to the gloom, the lack of contrast in the fading light creating a strange white mist in the middle distance. Green slipped from the fresh spring leaves as if their chlorophyll was being sucked down into the soil, as if this and every night were its own winter. Around me pollards and underwood twisted into irregular shapes, more shattered metal and rock than anything alive.

I couldn't bathe in the enzymes floating out from the unconscious, benevolent beeches and hornbeams. Instead as I walked, the heels of my boots scratching against the ochre of the surface of the ride, it was the stranger stories that I had uncovered about the forest that began to take shape in my mind.

Once grim tales are absorbed, they like to choose their moments to rear up again. My mind was filled with those who had entered the forest never to return. The thin, crackling paper in the Epping Forest archive is covered in copperplate handwriting and fading type detailing the horrors that London had squeezed from its streets and concealed under the oaks and beeches. From the 1940s there was a police report of the abandoned corpse of a baby, wrapped in pages of the *Daily Express* and tied neatly with string. For centuries the forest was one of the most dangerous places near to London, ruled at night by vagabonds, highwaymen and other murderous rogues. This continues. One evening some years ago my cousin saw a sinister, unexpected light through the trees as he drove along Rangers Road. He thought better of investigating and read a while later of a brutal murder, a body dumped in the forest near where he'd been. From the late nineteenth century there's an account of a man who bade 'Good day' to a courting couple before walking on a little and, drawing a pistol, blowing his head off.

In her 1971 short story 'Vaster Than Empires and More Slow', the science-fiction writer Ursula Le Guin described a visit to a distant planet by a spacecraft that numbers among its crew a being called Osden, selected for the mission for his ability to empathise with non-human life forms. Constantly tuning into his colleagues' dislike towards him, Osden is a brittle character who ends up being sent into the forest to work alone. There, secretly attacked and left for dead by another crew member, his fear is picked up and transmitted back to him by the colossal organism that is, he realises, the conscious and interconnected forest. Remarkably, Le Guin's fiction appeared decades before theories about trees communicating and sharing information via networks of mycorrhizal fungi became accepted by botanists and biologists. Unable to escape the atmosphere of unease, the explorers accept Osden's offer to be taken into the forest and left there in a state of empathetic balance that, finally, extends to the other humans. The expedition leader wonders at Osden's actions: 'He had taken the fear into himself, and, accepting, had transcended it. He had given up his self to the alien, and unreserved surrender, that left no place for evil. He had learned the love of the Other and thereby had been given his whole self. – But this is not the vocabulary of reason.'

This vocabulary, our human language that seeks to explain the world, to rationalise it and separate ourselves from terror, fails in the face of the magnitude of the living, sentient forest. In her introduction to the text, Le Guin writes that 'We all have forests in our minds. Forests unexplored, unending. Each of us gets lost in the forests, every night, alone.' The wiring of the forest into our awareness of dread comes not merely from the legacy of some primitive terror, but from a time when we had not yet developed the consciousness that separated ourselves from the forest, from nature. What animal knows no fear? We were never at one with nature in some placid coexistence, but in unconscious acknowledgement that fear is itself part of the balance.

When depressed or battling deep traumas from

younger years the imagination is at its most vulnerable, and that turbulent spring had flooded my mind with self-doubt and loathing. There was no real barrier between these low-swooping thoughts and what I had been finding in the Epping Forest archive, and it started to rage uncomfortably inside me.

The not-quite silence and the draining of the rich colours of May started cleaving my anxieties to fantastical thoughts. My own vocabulary of reason liquefied into a babble of distorted images and panicked mutterings and I felt my mind begin to slip.

In the big city, the threats are simpler. I'm fortunate to be a fairly tall and broad-shouldered white male, and it's a privilege to rarely feel afraid on the city streets, at least as an adult. A couple of attempted muggings feel small beef compared to how the face in the pollarded nobble of that beech peered at me. I saw a man sat under Grimston's Oak wearing a balaclava and reading a book. It's not the pitch-dark that's hard work, but the suggestive gloom of the surrendering day.

Can forests laugh? I felt mocked as the trees' limbs twisted around me and the ride grew ever fainter in the dimness ahead. My eyes itched with pollen and sweat and tears. I thought of how the Victorian popular press made a sensation of the clothes of the discovered dead and imagined what such a report might say about me: *Adult male late thirties . . . walking boots, polyester trousers, Farah, white cotton shirt, army surplus smock . . . spare phone battery . . . rucksack contained only a scuffed birthday card and in his hand he grasped a map.*

A couple mooched past content and unconcerned as

I lingered in the temporarily comforting light of the Fairmead glade, watching a thrush gabble away up and down the scales. It sounded deranged, cursing and mocking and warning me that from up there on its perch it could see the night coming to swallow me whole. Once back under the trees I couldn't stop twisting in all directions, eyes and ears straining, hearing voices that would turn out to be joggers who sweated past me, talking loudly about a mate's weekend away. As they vanished into the distance two muntjac deer pattered out from behind a holly and peered at me beneath tiny devil horns. My anxious breaths sucked in the vegetable taste of the new leaves and the bark, the muck, the pollen. The forest was inside me. I was starting to lose control.

I didn't want to be under these trees any more. I could hear things falling, rustling, creaking in the gloom far to the edge of the ride. At that moment I hated the forest, this forest, all forests, and felt as lonely and remote from myself as if I had been abandoned a thousand miles from my borrowed home. Breaths became coughs that turned into choked bile at the back of my throat. I was desperate to get out, yet I was more afraid of the smaller paths heading off the main ride than I was of keeping to it. I knew that to the left of me lurked the worn ramparts of the old Iron Age fort of Loughton Camp, said to be haunted. Perhaps down in the valley to the right Kind Kitty the hermit had never left the forest and still walked it.

As I thudded along and the path rose through Debden Slade I felt something dragging at me, urging me to turn and look to the right. The last blackbird might have been startled to hear me groan as my eyes opened wide at the sight of a man wearing an orange coat on the edge of the void of the forest. He had his head in his hands as he sat motionless on a log. Drawn upwards by some terrible power, my eyes went to the tree and there, dangling from a bough above through the blackness, I saw a line of light rope ending in a noose.

The rational part of my brain that would perhaps normally tell me to blink and look again or to give at least a friendly shout of 'Evening' to see if the man was OK was dissolved in a flood of adrenaline and panic. Chilled sweat soaked my shirt and blood pounded under my hair, which tingled as if it was trying to drag the skin off my skull and up into the trees, and I could see myself as if from just above, running past the slowly uncurling fingers of the new ferns as the night poured around me like foul smog.

I never looked back, but in my mind I saw the figure rise from the log and place the noose round his neck. I pegged it to the top of the hill onto Earl's Path, down over the gravel through the gorse past Baldwin's Pond and up, up, up the hill towards the luminous street lights of Loughton.

I was reeled back down to earth as soon as my feet hit the tarmac. I was panting, my shirt sodden, my lungs hacking with the exertion, the adrenaline draining from me as an uneasy calm returned. The forest had taunted me.

I wondered why I couldn't stride proud, pompous and male through the forest night like so many men do

and have always done. Forests feed into so many expectations of masculinity – the lumberjack, the woodman,
the hunter, the nature poet, the explorer, the conquer-
or of territory, aggressive dominion over nature. The
male interaction with place is transactional, wanting
something from it, whether that might be timber or
enlightenment, but I couldn't find that for myself. I felt
envious of Fred J Speakman, whose 1965 book *A Forest
by Night* details the hours he spent sat in a tree watching foxes and badgers while pondering about nature and
the meaning of things. The man who lived in the forest,
he seemed alright; night after night sleeping in the tent
at the heart of his camp, he had broken the prison of
fear of the dark.

As the pavement clicked under my feet I wondered
what it was that in some little-explored part of my
imagination had reached out and formed an alliance
with the living forest. Or perhaps I hadn't seen anything
at all. I stood and peered over the street to the large
detached houses, the expanses of brick drives leading to
the ostentatious pillars that hold up mediocre porches,
and into beige living rooms, the flickering HD screens
mounted on the walls and the people sat within, raising nightcaps to tight lips. The forest had spat me out,
but suburban Loughton was just as unwelcoming. The
people inside those houses felt as unreal as the figure
that I had left behind me. Who was he? I wondered
again, and aloud. I took out my phone to Google 'missing person Epping Forest', but as I did so it buzzed
with a FaceTime call from my sister, in the maternity
ward of a hospital in Auckland, New Zealand. During

my nerve-jangling rampage she'd given birth to a son. The brightness of my iPhone screen drowned out the twilight on the edge of the forest so that there was just the familiar face of my sister and this squished blob of her new boy and, in the periphery of my vision, the now unthreatening trees.

Across 11,000 miles of space and sea we talked as I walked to the Gardener's Arms, only streets away from where our parents grew up. From just outside the pub my granny would watch the flames rise over London's docks during the Blitz. With a rush of sentimentality hard on the heels of the receding panic I held up my phone so that the baby could see – or at least sense – this view of the city, glittering blue, red and orange from the forest which was once home to his family, wanting the place to flash in through that tiny camera and the circuits of the device up to the telephone mast and the satellites and then back down again, so that it might become a part of him, that he might understand it all from birth in a way that had seemed to fail me for thirty-six years. But he was otherwise occupied feeding. Unaware and blissfully alive.

11

Caught

Sat in the kitchen of my friends' house, I felt a rush of emotions as a few glasses of wine levelled out my racing brain – joy at the birth of my new nephew, a surreal gratitude that I was no longer under the trees where my mind had performed somersaults. But most of all, this nagging worry that I was in my late thirties yet still prone to an abject paranoia that had me fleeing the forest from ghosts and terrible threats in human and imagined form. I lay on my rough mattress in the dusty loft that night, staring at the square of light pollution above me, and, unable to sleep, started to unscramble memory. If I was starting to wrestle my sexuality away from the judgement of God, then why was I still consumed by a self-loathing that could turn at any point to self-immolating fear?

It was men that were at the core of all my terrors, I knew that. School and the violent pubs of St Albans and later Norwich had left me with a deep distrust of the burly white male. I didn't understand their language, their coded banter, their obsessing over the minutiae of football teams or cars, the weird dynamics of the group, with its peacocking, power structures and physical back and forth that are a poor substitute for emotional connection. In most things men did there seemed to be the threat of violence.

I had moved to London to forge my own identity and a life in a community where that kind of gruff masculinity was barely encountered, though whenever I left the capital for rural or small-town boozers I still felt nervous when I approached a busy bar. I knew it was a residual fear of those kids at school who liked nothing more than to throw a random winding punch at someone punier than them.

After a forest walk I nearly got a kicking from a pissed git in a Loughton chippy who got up in my face and barked through his lager fog, 'Where you from, poof?' and was only talked down by telling him my folks were from round the corner.

On an evening just before the summer solstice I'd gone bat-hunting and had had to run away from a group of lads whose aggressive shouts had disrupted the beeps of the bat monitor. When they spotted us through the dusk they'd asked, 'You alright mate?' in a tone that signalled they weren't asking a question and always spells trouble. I felt ashamed at my instinct to run. I had never really understood masculinity as it was expected of me, by religion, by straight or gay culture, and when I felt anxiety in the forest it was often through my failure to handle it appropriately as a confident man.

Deep within this I continued to come up against a

buried moment that had more of an impact than any laddish taunt or town-centre fist could ever cause.

Perhaps if my experimentation with Tippex Boy twenty-odd years before had resembled the tender myths peddled in coming-of-age films, things might have been different for me. I wished it had consisted of nervous kisses that deepened into lust in a bedroom covered in posters of pop stars, or in some empty locker room or secluded space. But the extreme risk of being caught cock in hand by teachers or classmates had created an association in my mind between sexual pleasure and danger. Adrenaline and testosterone can be drugs like any other. And I was hooked.

I spent the weeks after the desk-bound affair with Tippex Boy ended fraught with sexual frustration. Having a relationship with a girl was an abstract concept – it'd been earlier in my fourteenth year that I'd been reading a magazine about aeroplanes in WH Smith and, looking up at the sound of laughter, had seen a group of girls my own age pointing at me and mocking me. I just wasn't the type of boy that girls fancied, and anyway I never met any. I wasn't going to find another boy at school, either – the hetero terror had everything far too locked down for that. After my first queer experience the cruel masculinity of the boys around me felt even more pronounced – the way they'd throw a penny in front of one of the frequently persecuted kids and shout 'Jewboy' when he picked it up, the Chinese burns and ruler welts, the stealing and smashing of precious objects kids had brought in from home.

In the showers Tippex Boy's eyes no longer wandered

and he got dressed fast, turning his body away from me. I felt ashamed at his rejection, and if I was alienated at school before it was even worse now. At the last bell I'd leave as fast as I could to go to town.

It was on one of those trips that it first happened, on a Wednesday afternoon in the public toilet behind Marks & Spencer's. He had come up to me as I stood looking at CDs on a market stall. He wore blue, a cheap suit. He wasn't dressed that dissimilarly to me, really, in my black trousers, grey jumper and blue blazer. We might have worn similar outfits, but he must have been four or five times my age. He asked me where the nearest toilet was, and as soon as the words were out of his fat little mouth I knew what he wanted. I said I'd show him the way.

We didn't speak as we walked, although my mind was being ripped in two – the rhythm of *run run run* in my head not quite as loud as the voice telling me to go on. I had to slow down to match pace with him. Time went into a sickly motion. His rolling, pudgy body had its own gravity that I couldn't escape, dragging me out of the drizzle in the autumn twilight, through the door and into the sour, antiseptic air of the toilet. His breathing was heavy as we stood at the urinal, so heavy that strange noises started to leak from the back of his throat, *pop-hiss, pop-hiss, pop-hiss.*

His wet eyes stared down at my cock as soon as I pulled it out of the flies of my school trousers, and he grabbed it, starting to yank dry and hard, lips coming to mine like the eager beak of a baby bird. I was wise enough at least to know that I didn't want that to be my first ever kiss, so I knelt in front of him instead. He wheezed, rattling. The lights were painfully bright and I can still hear them humming now, still taste the Pears soap in my mouth. Perhaps embarrassed that he was too old to get hard, with some effort he clambered down onto the floor and started sucking me, but I couldn't feel anything, no pleasure, no nothing. All I saw was the desperate look in the eyes that gazed up at me, somewhere between surprise and ecstasy as a dribble ran down his chin. In that moment I had to stop him. I was terrified he might die there, sucking on my cock on the floor of a public lavatory. I pulled away, stammering, 'I'm sorry, I'm sorry, I'm sorry', and finally I could run, out of the toilet, down the alley and onto the high street where, as I turned to look back past the doors of M&S, I could see him lurching towards me. However useless I might have been at PE I managed to escape then, diving between two market stalls.

The way home was along the route I'd taken with friends to primary school. A few years before, aged nine or ten, we'd picked up pieces of charred wood from a bonfire on some waste ground and drawn black arrows on the fences to mark the way. Some of them were still visible and as I walked past each one, gasping from the headlong flight, each arrow might as well have stabbed me cruelly with the yawning horror that the child was lost.

At home I hurried up the stairs and lay on my bed, staring up at my model Spitfires and Messerschmitts hanging in frozen combat from the ceiling. I felt guilty, aroused, disgusted. Time seemed to have stopped, been cut off. The night before had just been another day after school, worrying about when PE was next to appear on the timetable and half-heartedly breezing through my homework. There was no going back to that.

I can't even remember how I knew back then that an old man asking a fourteen-year-old schoolboy how to find the nearest toilet was a proposition. There must be unspoken codes that go with the dynamics of exploit-ation that make for simple, easy traps. The terror when caught inside one was so pronounced that it changed me for ever. But that afternoon I was just a boy on his bed waiting for his mum to call him downstairs for tea.

That evening, sat with my family in the everyday normality of dinner, grace and leftovers, Dad being funny and me teasing my sisters, felt surreal. Had it really happened? It was so out of character and against anything that I'd been taught.

I took the memory of those two or three minutes, crushed it tightly and hid it deep within. It became my secret, and to stop it eating me I had to turn it into something special. I told myself this was a way of constructing a tough new exoskeleton to protect myself from the world.

The next day at school, and for a long time after, I felt different. I had something those other boys didn't. They might get drunk in the cathedral rose gardens and kiss some girl or other, but I had been desired by an adult. I had done something shocking and strange that they, with their anxious adherence to the codes of the lad and terror at being anything other than proudly straight, would never have dared to do.

It was a secret buried so far within that the memory became split off from the rest of me. That furtive school-uniformed creature of the public toilets took on his own life. Meanwhile, my public self went along with things for the next couple of years pretty much as they had gone on before. I still loathed sport and cried in Mum's arms every day before PE. I sat at home and drew blueprints for future navy ships and fighter planes, sketched mountain ranges and forest fires, obsessed over maps. But even these forests and lakes, mountains and rivers that had shaped the innocent years immersed in *Swallows and Amazons* started to become sexualised.

Two years later, aged sixteen, I took part in a school camping trip. It's clear from reading the rather obsequious expedition diary in my log of a trek through the Welsh mountains that I developed a massive crush on Will, the funny and buff instructor. On the same weekend I first kissed a girl. We realised that our sleeping bags had a universal zip and spent a night in a cocoon on the hard youth-hostel floor, hands down each other's pants and snogging with inexperienced tongues that by the next morning had given us both beards of crusted saliva. A few weeks after that I was temporarily distracted from pursuing her to become my first girlfriend when, after a sailing class, I glanced up and saw a fellow sailor peel off his tight wetsuit to flop out an unexpectedly big dick. Once again, I had to turn to the wall and change in a hurry.

I spent three months that summer with Vicky. Whenever the sun shone we'd lie in parks or fields with little to say but lots to kiss. It was always better outside than in my bedroom, where I'd be constantly distracted by the terror that Mum might come in when my hand was somewhere it shouldn't be. We went to our first gig together. Halfway through a snogging session during one of the less interesting bands she told me that she'd decided she wanted to have sex. I went to the venue loo and, flushing red and fumbling, bought a pack of condoms from the machine. We kissed our way through the headline band and kissed our way through the train trip back. We kissed our way across the road to the park that was just next to the station, and in the hot July air we climbed over the rickety fence that smelled of dog piss and slid down the slope on the other side. We kissed our way across the park, getting as far as the swings before we fell on each other and to the ground. She pulled my trousers down, climbed on top and pushed me inside her, but compared to the bloody rush of that fraught moment after school I could feel nothing. I wasn't there. I might as well have been floating up among the distant stars that prickled the sky above the park. I was with *him*.

12

Stoodley Pike

I have a painting of St Luke's Hospital in Bradford, where I was born and swiftly nearly died. It was made by one of Dad's church congregation, a schizophrenic and alcoholic. I suppose you could call it outsider art, but for me it's like the Epping Forest print or Granny's painting of High Beach Church, another talisman I've not been able to lose, always ready to transport me back into an imagined memory of a life that could have been, a nostalgia for what never was.

In the painting, executed in greys, greens and blues, the walls of the hospital are off-kilter and out of proportion, and the perspective is such that it emphasises the hills rising above the buildings of the city. In Halifax, where we moved when I was two, I loved how the moors looked from my bedroom window, smoke drifting in the firing of the heather, or topped by sparkling white in the colder winters. A group from our church would walk five miles of the Pennine Way every fortnight or so, where untrustworthy weather swept past us towards a horizon cut only by dry-stone walls that gave me, for the first time in my life, an awareness of how tiny I was compared to the vast and living world.

The Stoodley Pike monument has stood on the ridge of the Pennines above the Calder Valley towns of Todmorden and Hebden Bridge since 1856, a thick finger of gritstone pushed from the moorland into the wind. It stands at thirty-seven metres high, and a square base of four stone piers with an octagonal surround carries the huge stone obelisk. It was created by James Green, a local architect and Mason presumably responsible for the Star of David and set square and compasses carved into the dark stone. Stoodley Pike looks both grimly phallic and magical, dominating the horizon for miles around. From a distance it's impossible to tell how big it might look close up, and for me it grew in size as my memory of it aged.

I'd last visited in the mid-1980s, shortly before I moved with my family to the south of England. Our church group trudged through one of those thick, drizzly days the Pennines do so well, stone, rock and heather smeared together under clouds that gnawed at the tops of the moors. I was only seven at the time, but I can still vividly recall the black tower looming over me. Built from the same stone as the towns of the valleys of the West Riding, including the house I grew up in, it became a monument within my mind, a memorial to a lost sense of belonging that kept me anchored to the county of my birth.

Once we'd moved down to St Albans, my West

Yorkshire accent quickly vanished into the tarmac of the school playground where I'd sit, always listening for the northern wind. I imagined I heard it in the distortion of airliners flying far overhead, jet engines that left white contrails in the sky and a roar that dissipated to a whisper over 30,000 feet. I'd close my eyes and imagine the hollowed-out noise as a strong westerly, massaging a trillion blades of moorland grass. The sound took me back to that line of the tops outside Halifax, defined but irregular against occasional blue skies like a worn old blade. It cut through to expose flashes of memory: 'put wood in th'ole' for 'shut the door'; Dad packing a shovel into the car on winter drives across the tops; crocuses in the snow on roadside verges. Through this valley of a nearly forgotten past ran the Calder Navigation to Hebden Bridge, where Dad caught trout that tasted of mud and I'd watched a swan take hissing umbrage to an old man. It chased him down the towpath, his wife in hot pursuit trying to thrash the bird with her umbrella. This was the incoherent and romanticised compendium that made up the Yorkshire of my unreliable memory. I missed the place terribly. Even the theme music and opening sequence of *Last of the Summer Wine* became painfully evocative. Moving down south had given me the first real sadness that I had known, an awareness that our lives are not always in our control. In my case, due to Dad's job it was God who had sent us away from what I considered to be home, Caesar the ancient goldfish slopping in his tank in the trailer behind the car. I dreamed of returning to the landscape where I was born, and each night would earnestly pray for God to send a miracle Austin Maxi to carry me up the M1. It might well have been the first time I questioned His will.

My longing for Yorkshire ebbed and flowed over the intervening years. At its most heightened, I felt I might even form part of those moors. I'd had a succession of unpleasant operations in my earliest years and sometimes wondered if those pieces the doctors removed had been shovelled into the incinerator of Halifax Royal Infirmary to be burned with bandages and foetuses, puss and other bodily ooze. I dreamed the ashes whirled up the hospital chimney into a cold Yorkshire easterly, out of the town where the fields and dry-stone walls rise towards the dry white grass, before floating down past the stones of the monument to disappear into peat.

A few years before Alice and I broke up, during another period where the conflicting binaries of sexuality were threatening to disrupt my life, I'd experienced an intense pang of awareness that I needed to return. Back to the time before I had been touched by unwanted hands, when all the potential I'd had as a little boy was pristine and still alive.

I'd escaped the city to walk on my own down the Pennine Way from the village of Grassington to the limestone pavements above Malham Cove. It had been my first trip to Yorkshire in over a decade. As I got off the train and crossed into a sheep-cropped meadow, my tongue and eyes and nose had blown the door to the vault of memories, offering me a glimpse of the treasured happiness of my Northern childhood.

Now, as I drifted around London increasingly unsure of who I was and without a place to call my own, the

Calder Valley returned to the centre of my thoughts as it often did during times of crisis. Yorkshire flats were cheap to rent. There was an arts and music scene there that seemed far more weird and exciting than anything that was happening in London. As I searched the internet for train tickets and advice on wild camping I developed a fanciful notion that along England's Pennine spine I might find the roots of my own nervous system, that if I touched the stones of Stoodley Pike they could call me back.

Again I took the train to Grassington, but this time I struck out south across the moors down towards Hebden Bridge. At first the going was heavy. London life is easy on the feet, but the long, steady ascents soon forced my breath to come in rasps as the bright and hideous rucksack that held my tent and clothes for the weekend weighed heavy on my back. The day was unexpectedly hot. The air was thick. My chocolate melted. A Jack Russell yapped after me. Its owners were a weird pair, mother and son I think, and they stopped for a long and meandering conversation as their dog jumped up at my bag, tantalised by the scent of beef jerky. They went their way and I mine, onwards up the hill.

The ascent was endless and tedious, a forty-degree slope along a dry-stone wall, and it made my back and calves ache. I felt my stomach, podgy from too much ale, bulging over the nylon material of the rucksack's straps cutting into my skin, bringing back an all too familiar disgust at my own form. Walking was the only exercise my body could ever enjoy, yet it didn't seem to offer my mind any escape. Sheep stood stock-still in the mud and looked on as I stomped up the slope, all red-faced grimace and sweat, cough and wheeze. Fuck the sheep. Fuck the hill, covered in turds and purple-headed thistles that bobbed as if in laughter. Fuck the rugged proper Yorkshire waller bastards who were able to carry this stone and pile it up and be pleased with their good day's work. On the OS map, a blue pint pot in Lothersdale pinpointed relief. Fuck the map for that matter, and all the cartographers who tempt us on these fool's errands.

Dizzy under the sun and palms blotched with de-hydration, I panted my way in through the door of the Hare and Hounds. 'Boots,' came a grouching voice from the gloom inside. 'They're not muddy,' I replied, twisting and holding up the soles for inspec-tion. 'Right,' said the landlord, a face of grumpy indifference materialising as my eyes adjusted to the shadowy interior. At the bar, decorated only with a framed photograph of Paul Weller, I asked for a pint of lime and soda. The landlord looked at me and picked up a glass. 'Cheapest pub int' village,' he an-nounced as he handed over the drink, but the comment wasn't addressed to me. I gulped the water furiously, a carbonated fusillade clearing my tongue. 'Aye, most expensive too,' came a reply from the other end of the bar. 'Well,' said the landlord, 'it'd depend what you're after.'

Refreshed, yet perplexed by my encounter with a dour Yorkshireman straight out of central casting, I left the pub and struggled on up some steps set into the far side of the valley. A lady sat outside her cottage told me that the previous weekend walkers had trudged past through a blizzard, late for the year. 'You'll not be getting lost today,' she assured me.

Dotted along the Pennine Way are unintentional sculptures, bathtubs full of flowers and shrubs protected from grazing by thick mesh, a red diesel barrel in an old stone trough. Yet this haphazard appearance is an illusion, for however open the moors might seem, the landscape is one of boundaries. Long fences hummed, a black bin bag streaming from a garland of barbed wire. At one ruined farm the cratered eye of a half-decayed hare peered out from underneath a wooden door, as if it had been placed there as a warning. It made me feel uneasy, as did the sudden appearance of a man who'd been cutting peat a couple of hundred metres distant. He stopped what he was doing, resting on his tool, and stared at me, dogs prowling expectantly at his feet. It was unnerving to feel watched as I trudged over the flagstones towards the horizon slapped against the boiling grey sky.

The Moors Murderers were still a shadow that lurked over Yorkshire during the 1980s. Talk of their deeds must have reached my young ears, and I'd shrink from the car window while crossing Saddleworth Moor where mire and Myra alike might drag little boys down. Echoes of that long-forgotten dread started to filter through now and I anxiously kept looking back, afraid the man might be following me.

I was glad to reach one of the walls that cross the moors in lines as straight as the white scores the jets of my childhood left in the sky. I climbed the stile, stopping at the top to rest, and looked down the line of high-piled stones that it traversed. To the right, cropped grass pockmarked by tussocks shimmered green. I turned round and, in the split second before I jumped, saw Stoodley Pike floating in the hazy distance over the near horizon. I landed with a thump on the wild side where rough heather slid between purple and brown. I looked up, but the monument had vanished.

There were still three ridges to go before I reached it, a lengthy plod over the muddled patchwork of ground burned for grouse, wizened grey stalks like the fast-food chicken bones discarded on the streets back home. Eventually, the moorland gave way to mossy oak woods crossed by streams that ran over rocks the colour of rust, and I knew that not far away was Hardcastle Crags, a steep valley full of old trees that lurked in my woodland memory. But that wasn't my goal, not today, and I stayed on the Pennine Way, winding down past gardens where gnomes and sheep skulls sat among the daffs.

As I reached high points of ridges along the way south, Stoodley Pike doubled, then tripled in size. I crossed the Calder and its canal and had only the final slope to go. My friends in Hebden Bridge called and offered to give me a lift but I didn't want to cheat, even though I'd taken my last sip of water before starting the final ascent. Parched and exhausted, I trudged on towards the monument. At first Stoodley Pike was a dense black silhouette against the luminous afternoon sky, but, as I hauled myself up the final stretch, the sun sat just behind it and the old stones disappeared into light.

I passed under the hexagram carving through a doorway I'd forgotten existed and climbed the thirty-nine damp, mossy steps to the viewing platform. It felt strange to be there, halfway up this totem that had called out to me for so long. I hadn't remembered being able to climb it at all. I looked out across the endless drab carpet of the moors towards clouds not quite whipped into rain above a group of wind turbines and felt the distinct pang that accompanies an anti-climax. Three decades of wondering what this would feel like – and it didn't amount to much at all. I had had no revelation. The walk had been haunted by the same anxieties that I couldn't seem to shake. The little boy who'd been here no longer existed. He might as well have been claimed by the bog.

It seemed my past was defined as much by my present and fears for the future as by fickle memories. A newspaper article I'd read a few weeks before pooh-poohed a private school's bid to instil 'Yorkshire grit' in its pupils. 'You can't teach grit,' it ran, 'you imbibe it like mother's milk from your surroundings ... and once absorbed, it never goes away.' I wasn't so sure. As rocks become hewn stones, we move from our place of quarrying and will never quite fit again. As I leaned back against the cool side of Stoodley Pike my ears picked up the rhythm of the rattler train making its way along the Calder Valley. In fifteen minutes or so it'd enter Halifax through a tunnel under my primary school. I had long thought that, had I stayed in Halifax, I'd have grown up a confident teenager, being all a Northern boy should be. I knew now that this had always been impossible. The same discomfort at my masculine self would have reared its head here too, as would the gouging battle between faith and sexuality. Both were part of me, whether my house was of millstone grit or London brick.

Starting to feel the cold wind that blew over Stoodley Pike, I berated myself for my own foolishness in becoming gripped by a naive belief that nostalgia was ever anything more than a dangerous fog upon the present. Tomorrow I would take the train to Leeds and on to London entirely unchanged. I'd not found anything up there on those wide, empty moors because I'd not let the entirety of my adult self, the knots and gnarls of it, come up with me. There was much more work to do.

The clouds began to clear as I made my way down, throat clacking with thirst. Keen to reach my friends, I left the path to follow a compass bearing down into the valley, and promptly squelched to my ankles in the damp muck around a spring. The water babbled out into a stone trough sunk into the ground. I cried out dramatically and went down on my knees, flung water over my head, then dunked my face and greedily slurped from the surface. I stood and licked the water from my lips. It was cold and earth-sweet but salty from my sweat, and my eyes stung, blinking against the low sun. I stared into the light as the wind chilled my cheeks and tickled my ears with that familiar quiet cry as it rushed past, to where I did not know.

13

Behind Eagle Pond

Depression can feel cruellest in the early summer, when London's parks begin to fill with laughter from lunchtime and into warm, heady nights. That incident in the toilet behind Marks & Spencer's was over half my life ago but its horrendous consequences were still being felt, exploding the possibility of a positive future. I'd recently started seeing someone new, and however well it was going I found myself in a state of constant dread that I'd still not found a way to negotiate with the incoherent voices of my desires. I was with a woman again, but I knew that at some point my confusion as to how best to live a bisexual life would insist that I wasn't entirely fulfilled and send me off in search of a fleeting empty moment with another man.

Shortly after returning from Yorkshire I'd finally found a more permanent place to live, but it didn't bring the calm I longed for. I struggled to get out of bed in my newly rented room as the hot sun stewed the fug of night sweat and mildewing coffee dregs in discarded mugs. The bright morning light outside the bedroom window glared through the white blinds, turning them into cold slabs that trapped me indoors. One morning there was a thump as a swift slammed into the glass. I could hear it flapping and screeching in terror on the pavement outside.

Often on days like that I'd give up and remain listlessly at my desk, barely able to work. For a while that morning I pottered hopelessly around my room wearing one sock, the tick of my alarm clock methodically counting down another wasted day.

Eventually, with superhuman effort, I packed a rucksack with an apple and sandwiches of homemade bread and cheese (the wholesome things, though by now it was way past lunchtime), and made it out of doors. I planned to walk the full length of Epping Forest, hoping that conquering the territory might ease the tension I was feeling between the nervous start of a new relationship and the desire to continue in the promiscuous abandon of post-break-up single life.

I'd chosen to start my walk at the more urban southern tip of the forest, hoping that unfamiliar sights might help shift my all too familiar mood. Taking a lungful of traffic fumes and turgid summer air and trying to set my mind straight, I stepped over the rough vegetation at the edge of the road by Forest Gate Station and strode out. Heaps of freshly mown hay were scattered across the Centenary Path, golden in the sun and green in the shade. The ground looked bare around these islands, and the short stubble was strewn with litter. I nearly trod on a road-killed fox, its eyes and tongue rotted to nothing, the ruddy-brown fur blending with the grass, its flesh, blood and organs already dissolved into the earth. A discarded crisp packet sat just above its head, pricked up like an artificial ear. The bear on the label of an empty can of strong Polish lager growled up from a patch of mud next to a pair of pink panties that would have looked as if they were spread out for drying were it not for the crotch ripped by the mower's blade.

On the far side of Wanstead Flats the forest is crossed by a huge and noisy A-road interchange. The tunnel beneath it was full of crap and artificially lit even in the middle of a summer's day. As I squinted into the sun on the other side, the snarl of the traffic above my head, what had been a quiet niggle started to get louder in the back of my mind. It was a thought that I'd tried to suppress – this was to be a purposeful walk, wholesomely fuelled by sandwiches and apples – but it was becoming harder to ignore as I left the subway and walked back onto the Corporation's forest land. On the map I was just a few centimetres from Eagle Pond, adjacent to Epping Forest's most popular gay cruising area. I ought to go and have a look. In the interests of research, of course. But my mind that day was no sanitised laboratory.

I wonder when this part of the forest became established as a place for men forced by law and religious prejudice into twilighting their sexuality to find a knee-trembler under a hornbeam. How does Mother Nature call out to her dear boys? The first record I can find in the forest archives is a 1931 request to remove a hollow oak in Wanstead, lest it start being used for 'objectionable practices'.

I wonder who was first to queer this landscape. It might have been long before the Epping Forest Act when two men passed each other with a brisk 'Morning' and noticed an urgency in widened pupils that signalled more than a polite greeting. They'd have paused on the path, the gentle sweetness of the vegetation and the birds receding as desire took control. I wonder what bravery it must have taken to slowly look back, to see if he was still there. Who was the man who led the way into a thicket, hoping that he might be followed but sick to the guts in case his pursuer might be a keeper, a thief or a psychopath? Was it clerk, pauper, soldier or woodsman who first felt the surge of excitement when his reaching hand encountered both stiff cotton and cock?

In a BBC programme called *Forbidden Britain*, former teacher Paul Lanning told researchers that before the Second World War, when gay sex was years from being legalised, Epping Forest's notoriety was already widespread. He was a regular cruiser at Eagle Pond because there was 'no alternative', and admitted that what he saw there was shocking. 'Roman orgies ... it was ugly in the extreme,' he said, going on to describe the shame that he felt, forced into the undergrowth by the societal prejudices of the time. 'You were always discontented when you left the place, always ashamed of yourself. It was very, very risky, absolutely promiscuous ... trousers down, cocks up, cocks in ... masturbation, sodomy, sucking.' There's a sad triumph in Lanning's telling of his 'chief achievement' in the forest – the time

he managed to seduce a police officer who would ordinarily have been out to prosecute him. I wonder how
much has really changed since the 1930s.

In our supposedly liberal age, it's all too easy to forget
the ingrained prejudice, loneliness and social isolation
that force queer men to seek out places like Epping
Forest and make them their own. With a cock in the
mouth the modern world vanishes and, hidden from
God, we rut once more with Vico's giants. If even the
origin of the word 'forest' stems from ideas of outsiders
and renegades from the civilisation of the city, there
is, as well as the practical offering of concealment and
cover, a symbolism in queer men using these places in
rebellion to the society that rejected them. Societal and
religious repression have within their terrible power a
pressure that pushes queer men into promiscuous sexuality under the cover of the woods.

Yet I wasn't in the closet. I was out as bisexual to
all of my friends. I met plenty of men through work, at
gigs and clubs, though the only ones I ever developed
romantic and emotional attractions to always seemed
to be straight. I didn't *need* to go to Eagle Pond, or
anywhere like it. Yet within me was a powerful drive
that knew places like this were out there, never more
than a bus ride away, and I struggled to resist them.

The Centenary Walk had been set out to mark the anniversary of the saving of the forest, and was marked on
the map in bright green. But I peeled off, heading down
a side path lined with tall bushes of gorse and blackberry
bramble. The grassy way curved to the left, a channel
bundling me along. I wanted to be led. My hands tingled.

Blood racing. Drunk on desire. A man waddled in the other direction and though I refused to meet his gaze I knew it was fixed upon me. Now out to a bit more of a plain, the pond to the right, behind it the roof of Snaresbrook Crown Court. I wondered how many men over the years had found themselves being punished for what they'd got up to in the bushes not far away, a judicial system that has been as homophobic as it frequently still is racist, administering cruel punishments of hard labour or chemical castration for what later became, in tabloid and divorce-proceedings vernacular, 'a moment of madness'.

It's the discarded soggy tissues that give these places away, white splotches against the undergrowth. Horny Hansels need only follow the trail to find what they're looking for. Momentarily managing to find some calm, I told myself that I was there only for research, and walked (map in hand, a fine alibi I thought) in under an oak.

It was a Monday afternoon; I wasn't expecting to find anyone there, and wandered around taking photos on my iPhone. There were condom wrappers on the forest floor, one ripped in two between the LO and VE of its branding. In a moment fraught with genuine danger there wasn't much inclination to follow the request on posters nailed to trees by an organisation called OWL – Out With Litter – encouraging people to take their sex waste home.

Who has time to collect his rubbish when he's human prey out there in the bushes, vulnerable to police, forest keepers, homophobic gay bashers and muggers? An

Epping Forest keeper told me that one local took her aside, wanting to tell her why there were so many fires in the grassland around Eagle Pond. He said that 'It's people trying to burn out the gays.'

As well as a signal to other men, litter acts as a warning to everyone else, a territorial marker of a queer autonomous zone where heterosexuals might be advised not to tread. It also heavily genders the area, marking it out as a queer space, yes, but as an exclusively male one too. A friend who went to a local girls' school and spent many break times and after-school hours smoking weed in Epping Forest said they were always warned to stay away.

A bloke in a Tottenham Hotspur sports jacket walked past me, half looking at his phone. He headed under an elder and paused. I was well used to the coded signals, the furtive eyes, the brush of a hand against a crotch, the purposeful walk that slowed to a linger, but wasn't sure what he might be after. I walked away and stumbled into a pot-bellied man who was sitting on a log not reading the *Metro*. His intent was clear the moment he put his newspaper down, stood up and started after me purposefully, and I had to jink through the muddy tracks to lose him. Suddenly I was back in St Albans, side-slipping through the streets. Old skills die hard. It wasn't difficult to escape – the paths there are even more convoluted than the ones on the map of Wanstead Flats just to the south. But this was a private network, beyond cartography, beyond nature. It felt more like the warren of dank, meandering corridors and darkrooms that one can stumble into in a gay sauna. Little spurs disappeared off to end at trunks. Low branch overhangs were the roofs of sultry bowers that had clearly hosted fantastic, frenetic orgies.

I wasn't just the damp that started to make my breath feel heavy as I spotted a baseball cap through a gap in the bush. I approached. The face beneath the cap grinned at me. And grin he might – crouching on the ground in front of him two men were taking it in turns to suck his dick, wanking each other off as they did so. One wore a decent suit, the other the overalls of a painter. I smiled and carried on walking, fully intending to leave them to it. But this was a labyrinth created by desire, and compulsion can make you walk in circles just as much as the distracting randomness of any forest. I stumbled forwards, but a tunnel of holly swept me up like a fairground ghost train and brought me to a glutinous pop as a cock was hurriedly pulled from a mouth and four startled eyes turned to peer at me. I apologised for disturbing them, but the suckee beckoned. I shook my head and walked on.

I realised that everyone else here was in their civvies – sportswear, office clothes, jeans and so on – and in my walking boots, white shorts, white T-shirt, practical rucksack and with map in hand I must have looked out of place. I was conscious that despite the blood racing through my body I was a voyeur, and I felt guilty. I even felt that I was betraying myself by not indulging, not going in and feeling welcoming hands reach out for me. The old struggle between the familiar comforting desire for an intense encounter without words and loyalty to a relationship that had just begun screamed within me. I tried to look up towards the sun to locate west and the way out but I couldn't orient myself. I kept walking. I found a new clearing with an OWL sign broken in two on the ground, and the undergrowth opened up, like a curtain rising on the star of the show – a buff black man, gym bag slung over his shoulder. With a quick flit of the eye I spotted the curve of his long, thick cock through his grey jogging bottoms.

The forest around me vanished. I've read enough about the liberating, sensual power of drink or drugs entering the body of an addict to know that this is exactly the same experience. So many times before I had failed to defeat this impulse to absolute and abject loss of control. Sex might be even more powerfully addictive than any substance because it is so rooted in our human purpose, and here on this hot Monday afternoon in the forest the conflict felt more and more intense. 'You alright fella?' the man asked as I passed him. It wasn't a come-on. I squeaked something half in relief and half in disappointment as I stumbled on and out onto the road, north towards home, mind on fire, as confused as I'd ever been.

It's surprising that Epping Forest's lively cruising spots have endured as long as they have. The forest authorities are well aware of them. A keeper told me that their response is far less draconian than it would have been in the past. This is a welcome if stark contrast to Paul Lanning's experience in the 1930s, when 'police cars would come through and [the cruisers] would all be chased away like butterflies'. The keepers now collaborate with OWL and other local LGBTQI organisations to run litter picks and encourage those who use the area for sex to respect it more. 'The problem is that it's not gay men, it's straight men, or gay men leading a straight life,' one of the forest keepers told me. 'It's really difficult to tap into a community who refuse to believe that they exist.'

Millions of men must have endured double lives in which they rely on places like this for a release that allows them to be who they are for a fleeting, shaking moment. Part of the joy of big cities has always been that they create and sustain queer places in a way that nowhere else can. These are different worlds within the city, radical and remote from the ordered, asexual modern existence that goes on just a matter of metres away. They are places of pure intensity, the intimate urgency of transient human contact, a suck, jerk, fuck and then gone. They have an energy like nowhere else.

In his journal, published in 1991 as *Modern Nature*, Derek Jarman recounts the emerging sexuality of his youth as, decades later and HIV-positive, he tries to breathe life into the garden of Prospect Cottage in the inhospitable terrain of Dungeness. He writes beautifully about Hampstead Heath, London's most famous cruising area and Epping Forest's genteel western sister. Just like the forest, the Heath was saved for the people of the capital and remains controlled by the Corporation of London. Jarman describes the Hampstead cruising territory as almost resembling a garden party, 'people laughing and shouting, like a midnight swim'. Most of all he revels in the erotic potential of the place, writing one Christmas that he 'saw a naked boy marble white in the moonlight lying in the cleft of an oak tree, motionless in the freezing cold.' It's an echo of the climactic scene in his 1976 feature film *Sebastiane*, where tied to a wooden stake on an arid, rocky clifftop, the naked body of the Roman guard is pierced with arrows and hangs limp, blood and sweat dripping down to his cock. Jarman even made a film there, young men larking about, surrounded by trees as a saxophonist plays, the landscape both eroticised and a locus of rebellion against the oppression and prejudice of what Jarman derides as 'heterosoc'. I envy that freedom, and how he writes that 'once you are over that invisible border your heart beats faster and the world seems a better place'. For some, perhaps, that might still be true. But for how many men, dwelling forever in a closet with doors slammed shut by culture, religion and self-loathing, does that sensual netherworld become a hell? These might be places where closeted sexuality can for a moment be cast aside, but to step out from under those concealing boughs and return to the lies of domesticity and self-censorship can cause unbearable pain. In the flats and houses surrounding Eagle Pond, countless dinners cooked by dutiful partners have been digested after an aperitif of cum.

I loved how Jarman wrote about his times cruising. I know that I cannot enjoy them in the way that I might wish to, free of worry and high on the thrill. I have learned enough, however, to believe that they're vital for so many people unable to openly negotiate the difficult terrain of sexuality in a culture that still, especially for men, sees attraction as a binary choice. For thousands they still provide places of temporary escape from the suffocation of repression, for many more a simple and easy spot of fun on the way home from work or the pub. Good luck to them, these men who find so much in intensely private moments in collusion with the forests. I hope their pleasures are never taken away.

But for me they are troubled places, where the seclusion of the hawthorn bushes melts into tiles and bleached steel, and dappled sunlight the unflinching glare of electric light. However traumatic my experience with the snuffling ogre of the public toilet had been, I couldn't resist going back. Sexual experiences two, three, four and on were similarly coerced at the hands of grim predators for whom cruising areas were fertile hunting grounds, full of tender prey.

I encountered the second man in a toilet behind the civic hall, where in the autumn of 1991 the IRA had mistakenly detonated a bomb while setting the timer, scattering pieces of the terrorists all over the town centre. It was a familiar scenario, to walk into the damp concrete room, the air acrid with the aphrodisiac stench of bleach and piss, and know that the man stood at the urinal wasn't pissing. To start shaking with terror and desire as I stood next to him in my school blazer and looking down to see him stroking himself, long and slow with hairy fingers and a gold signet ring. To unzip my flies and then look up to meet a stare that froze me to the spot as the urinal flush sent water rattling loudly and he sank down to try to suck me and I shook in fear and zipped myself up. I ran as he shouted after me.

He followed. He always followed, that one. He never seemed to leave the town centre. Once in Our Price I felt uneasy while browsing the CD racks; I glanced up to see his glowering eyes locked on me from under thick brows and I ran out of the shop. I became adept at losing him by doubling back through the front and back entrances of shops. To make this cat-and-mouse game more bearable I would pretend that I was a spy.

My fantasies were not about the men themselves – I was drawn to them because they offered release, though I never once came. The encounters took place on the slimy floors of grotty toilets or after coy conversations in the park, me bold in my school uniform seven, six, five, then four and so on years shy of the then age of consent, with men whose eyes bulged and whose idea of a come-on was to lick their chapped lips at me. They were universally old and ugly, jerking themselves at me from under overhanging bellies. I never met anyone under forty, let alone my own age.

Another man told me he was a police officer, threatening me with arrest unless I went with him. I was too afraid and naive to resist and followed him to a toilet in an office building where I simply did what he wanted. As soon as he came he zipped up and shut the door behind him, leaving me naked in the cubicle and telling me to wait five minutes before climbing out of the window so we didn't attract unwanted attention. I stopped wanting to go to town with my mum or my friends in case we bumped into one of them.

I never told anyone about any of this. How could I? I had few friends and nobody to confide in. My relationship with Vicky had ended not long after we first had sex. I went away on a family holiday and while I was gone she hooked up with someone from my school. He was in the rugby team, and when I got back for the new term chanted taunts of 'Hey boy, he nicked your girlfriend' pursued me around the corridors at break times, along with his boasts of what he did with her in bed. I tried my level best to get on. Everything must have seemed to be as normal to my family, yet to them I was still a child. When in the midst of all this I failed my first driving test my mum tried to cheer me up by giving me a video of *Bagpuss*, the TV series about a soggy old cloth cat that I'd loved as a child. I burst into floods of tears, wishing I could go back to the time when her gentle voice singing the lullaby 'Jesus, tender shepherd, hear me' would make me feel so beautifully whole.

Now when I catch a side-eye at a public urinal or see a man sloping furtively through certain bits of Epping Forest the liberating promise of the cruising ground has become twisted. It's no longer a place of freedom. I look through the trees and there are the ghosts of those hungry men, feel them reaching out to drag me back to being that boy, afraid yet aroused, unzipping the trousers of his school uniform.

I didn't make it to the top of Epping Forest that day as I had planned. After the distraction of my ex-ploration around Eagle Pond I felt deflated and guilty that I had even been tempted to join in, not because of the act itself but because of someone I was starting to care a great deal about who was spending her Monday afternoon at work a few miles further into town. As the sun dipped to the west I took the train from Chingford back home for another disturbed night of sleep.

The next day I checked how far I'd walked using the Health app on my iPhone. It was much further than the kilometre squares of the map had suggested. The apple remained uneaten in my bag.

14

Teenage Lightning

I know a thing or two about compulsion, a misan-thropic autopilot suddenly taking control of my body and flying it into uncomfortable places and situations. I understand how these spirals run and how they end, ra-tional decision-making dissolving, the eventual collapse requiring months, sometimes longer, of nervous rebuild-ing before the internal violence returns. As the years went by I realised that this desire for high-adrenaline, risky sex had become a part of me. It was difficult to form lasting heterosexual or homosexual relationships as I roamed the landscapes between them, drawn to sexual territories defined by imbalances of power and extremes of experience. I struggled to be content with one or the other.

The sexually fixated imagination is all-consuming. It eclipses everyday things, the desire to live healthily, to nurture relationships with family and friends, to un-derstand what love can feel like. Even to know why I kept going to Epping Forest. Finding myself drawn to the cruising area, to feel the eyes of those men peering through the trees from a past over two decades distant, had undone everything I had loved about the forest as a child. It was then that I understood I carried them with me, unwanted, as if I were chained to their ghosts. They had been with me since I was fourteen, fifteen, sixteen, and they were with me now.

When you're always watched by the past it is impossible to be alone in the present. Immersing myself so deeply in the forest's chaos, feeling the tension between its trees and the city that surrounded it, had started to pull me apart. I couldn't go there to be cleansed by the trees and sigh winsomely through the gently lofting leaves of a summer's day because everything that had happened to me was there with me too. I began to realise just how much havoc kneeling before a man in that humming, brightly lit toilet and tasting Pears soap had wrought. For years I had tried to brush it off. When in my early twenties I finally started to tell close friends about what I had experienced, I did so via crude jokes about providing 'care in the community' services for OAPs.

There are so many myths surrounding the sexual abuse of teenage boys that understanding that you've been a victim can be a long, fraught process. It was, I always told myself, part of growing up. I never considered that I was a victim, despite the fact that when it all started I was seven years below the then age of consent for gay sex and that these men were old enough to be my grandfather. *I* had put myself in those situations after all. I had *wanted it*, even if what had started as curiosity soon turned to panic and then it was too late to escape. Although I was only fourteen when it first happened, I convinced myself that I was a man, not a child, and I had grown up in a society that told us that men don't get raped.

I found a keeper's notebook in the Epping Forest archive that set out in matter-of-fact yet grim detail a report of an older man who in March 1912 was spotted acting suspiciously with a fourteen-year-old girl. The keeper apprehended the pair and took them to the nearest police station, only for the male suspect to escape through the window of the gents. Like anyone else would I felt sickened to read it, but only later did it occur to me that almost exactly the same thing had happened to me.

The normalisation of exploitative sexual encounters between older men and young boys and girls is part of a long history of internalised victim-blaming. For all the juicy headlines about the various investigations in which major organisations have had to confess to sheltering sexual predators, they've not gone anywhere. Those men who used me had not found me via the exploitation of any formal position of power, but by being in their right place at my wrong time. It's hard, as a child or young teenager (if indeed the two are separate things), to understand that what's happening to you isn't normal. The abusers themselves are enabled by history, pornography and the obsession with youth that pervades every aspect of our society. Heterosexual and homosexual gay-porn sites offer up millions of hours of films that build fantasies around the loss of innocence, older men fucking girls in school uniforms or sports kits or on beds strewn with soft toys. Encountering films like these as someone who has as a young person fulfilled those very same sexual fantasies undermines the truth that what happened to you was an abuse of power.

Straight and gay culture share a tendency to fetishise youth, seeing early sexual encounters across a couple of generations as a rite of passage, something everyone does. The ancient Greek vogue for older men taking young lovers is frequently viewed with rather romantic eyes. Much as I admire Derek Jarman, I found a passage of his writing in which he lamented not being picked up by an older man during his teenage years distressing. And within Coil, the band whose music I dearly loved and who via their roots in Throbbing Gristle and my stay in Ian's house were intimately entwined with my experience of the forest as an adult, was something deeply problematic. Peter 'Sleazy' Christopherson was an accomplished photographer and took black and white shots of strikingly young boys, shirtless and holding knives against their soft skin. Coil's video for the track 'Love's Secret Domain' features young Thai boys (of legal age, of course) in loincloths dripping wax on their writhing bodies. Jhon Balance once introduced the eponymous song by saying, 'Teenage lightning is the energy generated when you rub two teenagers together.' With clarinet and marimbas rolling like sunlight over an English down at the height of summer, it's a stunning piece of music, an absolute favourite to this day; yet to listen to the lyrics was to feel both pleasure and exquisite torture:

Don't be alarmed it will not harm you
It's only lightning, teenage lightning
. . .
It's unbelievably real

Unbelievably real. What had happened that afternoon after school had become so unbelievably real that it had become hyper-real, the hidden desire that boiled beneath my outwardly normal exterior demanding to be heard.

Early sexualisation from abuse is thought by psychiatrists to have a devastating impact later in life, often leading to sexual addiction and an inability to form lasting relationships. I know why people are compelled to extremes of sexuality and find their pull so impossible to resist. It is silent, but it is always there. It might strike at any time of day, this sudden urge for a need to be met at any cost. It's easily appeased, and in a sexually saturated world it can be impossible to avoid the triggers to succumb. The internet makes it hard work too. You can be cruising for chat on Grindr at the flick of a finger, and enough pornography to last for the rest of your life is only a click or two away online. The jump from reality to indulgence is part of the thrill, the knowledge that in the city it can be satisfied if you know down which side roads to plunge, which urinals to wait at, which way to enter the park or the forest.

You might think you can spot an addict, notice the physical signs of their habit, the bloating, the reddened eyes, the shakes, the smell, the incoherence. But a sex addiction is harder to identify. And unlike alcohol or drugs, sex addiction is not binary. You could, I suppose, give up having sex altogether. Become celibate, avoid the erotic. You might as well try and stop drinking water. It would be to go against the fundamental purpose and great mystery of our bodies. It's ironic that the itch that feeds sex addiction is rooted in the destruction of emotional intimacy, choking love.

In the early days of Epping Forest, before the invention of powerful firefighting machines, huge areas would burn every year, entire habitats going up in flames in minutes. I often imagined the fire uncontrolled and following its own logic, sweeping through the grass and the scrub and into the trees, their branches crackling in hot orange destruction, the smoke curling and carving its way into the sky, and before long nothing is left but dust and charred death. This is what it feels like when you've once again given in.

As a teenager infatuated by the twisted romance of the city that I heard in pop music I had dreamed of going to London for the anonymity it would offer me to reinvent myself. Aged twenty-one I made the move happen by taking a terribly paid data-entry job down in Hammersmith. I immediately began to negotiate with the city the price you have to pay to forge a new self. London was a place where the opportunity for high-adrenaline sexual release can be found round so many corners, it was just a case of finding their secret portals. It's in times of frustration and repression that it becomes all too tempting to step through them, and when you've done it once it's easier to go back again and again.

The job was awful, dead-end work for long hours and low pay. I found myself in a deep spiral, from pub to fitful sleep to getting up early enough not to be too late into the grim office with its dirty, metal-framed windows and electronic hum. To the quiet pattering of keyboards filling the internet with numbers and our bosses' bank accounts with coins, my life slowly started draining away. It pushed me hard in the other direction. Alcohol and immersion in a new community of London's music world wasn't the only escape. Just as it had when I was a lonely schoolboy, compulsive sexuality provided another kind of outlet.

There were once Dilly boys who lurked in the alleys of the West End, willing to lose themselves to older men in exchange for a few coins. Now the commute home on the Piccadilly Line could provide me with cheap thrills via a quick flit out of the tube doors and up the escalators to the last remaining sites of seedy old London. Out at Green Park station and across the park to Marble Arch, down the network of subways to a toilet, a secret concrete cavern where a man with a cock tattooed and pierced and thick as a bottle leered at me through a broken mouth. Leicester Square, where pound coins pushed through slots would prompt peepshow women to put down their books and half-heartedly strip, or gay-porn shops down ancient alleys that offered then illegal hardcore videos if you knew the right way to ask. I could get out at Holborn and walk a block to Tavistock Square Garden, where one afternoon I let a man drop his gym kit and push me up against a tree with thick lips on the nape of my neck and hands up my shirt as a Bloomsbury Set walking tour reached their *Mrs Dalloway* climax on the other side of the gently wafting leaves. As his cock in a condom lubricated only with spit slid between my thighs and entered me, I had to bite my hand to not cry out and give us away. Or I might change to the Central Line and visit the urinals at Liverpool Street Station, a wanking wall of diverse masculinity. There was King's Cross and the musty confines of Oscars, the gay cinema. You'd be thankful it was dark before sitting down to watch the blurred digital porn on the screen, always remaining alert to bat away hands that reached across the grotty seats. And up at the end of the journey, at Finsbury Park itself, where the park gates opened all night like a maw and shadows moved under bushes and trees. I once saw a black man sucking off a Hasidic Jew in curls, traditional long black cloak and hat, which felt like multicultural integration of a sort.

Just as part of my compulsion to seek out these encounters with men in my teenage years had been an act of rebellion against the conservatism that surrounded me, so these after-work disappearances into the quiet sexual underworld of London were a kick against the mundanity of my day-to-day life. I possessed a power in my sexuality. The radicalism of Derek Jarman and Throbbing Gristle had taught me that. It's not to say that I never enjoyed any of this. The pleasure was often visceral and I relished being objectified. The power dynamics I was exploiting gave me a surety in my masculinity that I'd never known before.

My body was no longer something that I loathed, but a weapon that I could use to be adored, lusted after, craved. Men were no longer the bullies and sports bores of school or the emotionally stunted, violent lads of the Home Counties and Norfolk pubs, but erotic, anonymous creatures. These furtive queer worlds, both offline and on, were places where I felt I finally had sexual agency, a better place in the hierarchy. I was equal to those my age and, I came to realise, used my increased confidence to prompt a psychic redress or somehow get revenge on those who'd abused me as a teenager. Older and bigger, I knew I could taunt and tease, lure them in and suddenly and cruelly take myself away, denying them what they wanted. Besides, for every old git now left naked and slavering there were many more men of my own age who were attractive and very, very good at what they did. There was something delicious about slipping out of work on a break for a threesome with two rudeboys whose bodies were wound tight as springs and who became ferocious seconds after they were stripped. Yet using sexuality to bolster my confidence was a dangerous game. I was building myself up on a shaky foundation of religious shame and the high-stakes thrills I'd found with both Tippex Boy and the foul old men.

Relationships where sexual connections were made that weren't just fleeting but had at their core an enduring respect and love became increasingly tricky. For a while, years even, I was able to find some balance and peace, as I had with Alice. It was in those uncomfortable months after our separation, when I felt a freedom to use the alchemical power of complete sexual abandon to figure out who I really was, that my actions became habitual. Under societal pressure to be either straight or gay, I had thought that visiting these places to have sex with men was a symptom of a deeply repressed homosexuality. Exploring extremes with men and women, both in real life and in the even more deeply permissive anonymity of the internet, I might have found an honest fluidity in my desires, but it had become corrupted by compulsion. I found myself in situations that I wasn't enjoying but couldn't stop. I began to hear an insistent whisper telling me that deep at the heart of all this was something uncomfortable and sour. I had lost control.

I wonder if we victims of abuse show something in our body language that makes us out to be weak, vulnerable easy prey. There was a night-bus journey when a middle-aged man carrying a pungent kebab came and sat next to me, pulled out his dick and pouted and leered, and I was too afraid either to get off and run or tell the driver. It wasn't so long ago when, naked in the changing rooms after a swim, I felt that someone was watching me and looked up to see a fat little man holding his towel so the rest of the men couldn't see that he was jerking his stubby nothing towards me. His fish eyes glued me to the spot, stripping away the years, and half my age fell off me – I was back there again, my teenage self utterly vulnerable and exposed. I dressed hurriedly and ran out into the evening, feeling angry with myself for not having said something, for not having called him out or punched him on the nose.

That had happened just when my relationship with Mia was starting to become something more serious, when text messages would arrive and send the day fluttering along a little better than it had been before. We'd spend evenings off the booze drinking Greek mountain tea, gradually starting to talk about a future that might be shared. I couldn't bear to let on that, against all this, I was starting to fear myself. What if that man in the cruising area had pulled that huge cock out of his jogging bottoms in front of me, or the troll in the swimming pool had actually been young and hot? I didn't know if I could trust myself, because that impulse to get lost in anonymous sex was just a way back to that toilet in St Albans. That it had such a powerful hold on me, far worse than ever before, terrified me now. I started to think that perhaps that autumn day in the early 1990s wasn't the first time I had been caught. The more I researched sexual abuse, the more I wondered if something had happened to me before then that I subsequently erased from my conscious memory.

As a kid I never liked to stand up and pee with my back to a toilet door. I had a recollection that someone had told me a secret and insisted I not repeat it to my parents – a cliché of abuse, but a memory that had always been there. As a child I had constant dreams about being taken away by strangers to somewhere horrible.

Then, on a hot August night in my new room, a nightmare. I was standing at the top of a grass verge above a hollow in the landscape that was full of people. I felt a tug on my sleeve and looked down to see myself, familiar from a 1980s photograph in a blue jumper with my name on it that I think had been knitted by my granny. The figure of my younger self didn't smile as he held out a DVD for me but fell, rolling down the slope. He tried to get up but was surrounded by men who pulled down their trousers. I attempted to get down the slope but I couldn't reach him and as he disappeared I woke up screaming.

The next day was horrendous. It'd been such a brutal nightmare that I was sure there must have been something in it, a leak from a locked vault deep in my memory. I couldn't focus at work but just kept replaying the horror over and over in my head, along with the sequel that was only too real, the St Albans loo. That evening I couldn't hide my rotten state of mind and as I told Mia about it I sobbed, barely able to breathe. She held me and stroked my hair.

Like the forest itself the landscape of our memory is in a constant state of flux. It is highly subjective, and our dreams are too unreliable to offer evidence of anything. During the early 1990s a 'Satanic Panic' had taken hold and was all over the news. Children had accused their parents of bizarre sexual rituals, some of which were said to have happened in Epping Forest, not far from the home I shared with Alice in Walthamstow. Perhaps those false accusations were conjured from an unconscious memory of another event that occurred in Epping Forest, on its far side, near to High Beach, when a paedophile called Ronald Jebson kidnapped two children and hanged them from a tree. The press dubbed the case The Babes in the Woods murder, turning it into a real-life fairy tale. Maybe those ancient stories themselves come from the terrible things that men have always done to children under the cover of the woods.

When we are young we pick up these stories, often whispered not quite far enough from our ears by the radio or parents, or read about them in fragments of discarded newspapers. We're warned not to speak to strangers or get in their cars. These admonishments were no doubt conflated with the narratives of children wandering into woods and becoming prey to the gnarled deviants, witches and the like that are a staple of the fairy story and became lurid and real.

I may never know if my body was touched by some-one unwanted long before that gargoyle of a pensioner enticed me into the public toilet. His hands, whoever's hands, still exerted their chill grip. And I didn't know how to lose them.

15

When the Bough Breaks

A few years ago, on a twilight walk, I spotted something off in the woods. It was a shrine of sorts, little notes to a 'beloved daughter' in plastic sheaves, ribbons tied round a trunk and lumps of old candle wax on the floor.

There is a legend about a suicide pool, a malignant place somewhere deep in the forest that, according to the writer Elliott O'Donnell, lures people to their deaths: 'People who have been thought by their most intimate friends to have had no inclination to commit suicide have been found drowned,' he wrote in *Haunted Britain*. In 1959, *Essex Countryside* magazine launched a competition to find the pool. One person claimed to know the location but refused to divulge it, saying it was too evil. Another suggested it was the Wake Valley Ponds, where my dad would feel afraid when fishing at night.

I don't believe in the existence of a suicide pool in Epping Forest. It is only a supernatural cipher and deflection from the truth. The forest and the deliberate ending of life are and always have been close companions. The Epping Forest archive holds a litany of the dead. In September 1867, 'near one of the large oaks that are so well known', a man was discovered with 'the top of his head blown entirely off' by a home-made gun. On 12 January 1940 a corpse was pulled from Wake Valley Pond: 'The police believe this is the man who was reported missing about the middle of October last and who left his car by the pond side.' January 1940: 'on the 20th body found of PC Henry Marsden aged twenty-eight from Kennington policeman in Suffolk found dead in Burywood having hanged himself by a scarf'. Edith Mabel Bennett of 21 Anstell Avenue in East Ham 'drowned result of unsound mind' in Heronry Pond. In 1940 a woman was found in the Hollow Pond, forty-five or fifty years old, 'nothing by which to identify her'.

We do not need a mythology of siren ponds to explain away the possibility that lies within us all to conspire with a landscape to finish ourselves, and that nobody, not even those closest to us, might expect it.

You can die of an overdose, or the long-term effects of drug use. Alcohol is directly responsible for almost 10,000 deaths a year in the UK. A propensity for risky sex and disease aside, it is very hard to die of sexual compulsion – except perhaps by your own hand. While I can understand that my sexual compulsion was a response to some deep desire to recreate those early experiences of high tension with my school friend or, more grimly, at the hands of pederasts, the physicality of it is something I can describe but don't quite comprehend.

It can come on with the most insignificant trigger – the slightest flick of a butterfly's wing can cause a hurricane. The tiniest irritation, usually when my confidence plummets, can prompt my mind to start flailing in search of comfort. Some psychologists describe it as an obsessive trance-like state that, like a cult with a membership of one, relies on rituals – the bus journey where the release is just a few steps away into a concealing, cool, green place; the online sprees. The feeling that you deserve a reward after something going well at work, or conversely a fillip when it has gone awry. The delayed gratification of the hunt is often more rewarding than the moment itself.

It is my body that tells me I am about to lose it. I panic. A sourness flows through me, as if my fingers and toes are drawing some intoxicating power from the air. My stomach knots, a twist that makes my heart beat harder. In desperation, I might try to push away the impulse by conjuring the dreamed-of places of my childhood, to put myself in the back of an Austin Maxi looking out at the Yorkshire moors or the great grey of Norfolk's sea. But the memory disintegrates too quickly to rescue me. The physicality of those places couldn't save me either. The supposed wonder of nature was not enough to stop me lowering my eyes from the trees or whatever unfamiliar bird might be singing over yonder in favour of going online again to get lost in the rush of the hunt.

Sometimes the surge will suddenly retreat, hissing,

back into the subconscious. On the night of my birthday just after Alice and I broke up I came round from the trance semi-naked in a stuffy living room, mediocre porn on the telly, three flaccid men half-heartedly pawing at each other on a cheap creaking sofa bed as they eyed me up. With that peculiar adrenaline gone I had to leave, quickly putting on my clothes and escaping into the night.

Single, I was free to do what I wanted, but the liberation and the highs I had once felt from quick encounters were starting to fade: whether with men or women, they left me feeling cold and ever more alone, especially when I started to gravitate towards the murkier corners. I'm not sure when rock bottom is reached for those of us who are prone to sexual compulsion. There is always somewhere more debauched that you can go, a more extreme or visceral fantasy to be realised.

An older man, an architect and a dom, had wanted me to come back a second time to role-play a slave market, and told me he would have a 'nice n****r for you to inspect, boy'. There were women whose submissive desires meant trying to tap into an overly dominant masculinity that made me feel deeply uncomfortable. I had met a nurse on Tinder who wanted to call me Daddy and got pissed off when I refused to call her my daughter and say how lucky I was to be fucking her. I left her place at dawn and walked back across the marshes hungover and groggy as the sun floated garishly in the cold winter sky. Unsatisfied, I couldn't help but shield my phone from the brightness of the light as I once more returned to the hunt where I was both pursuer and prey.

It had gone on long enough for me to know that the feeling that descended afterwards was not shame that came from a fear of God. It was more like the worst hangover that I had ever known, the harmful toxins all manufactured by my own body. I sank into a place of self-hatred, absolutely rotten with emptiness and disgust. Wasted time, wasted mind, the wasted gift of my body to people who did not deserve it. However intense my fantasies were, whatever the combination of men, women, outlandish and orgiastic scenarios, the cycle became deeply boring. The inevitability of relapsing back into the old patterns, the endless repetitive chat on Grindr, the weary scroll through webcams or porn sites of men and women became stripped of any eroticism, or life. I'd catch my face reflected in the screen and could not recognise the pale, haunted eyes that looked back at me.

If I traced the thread of that feeling back through my life, I knew it all came from one source, one time, one man. The old jokes I'd made about pensioner care had stopped raising a bitter smile. He was surely dead by now, but he had me in chains from beyond his grave. He might even become my murderer.

I wonder what it takes for that little whisper of death to win the negotiation and break the bonds of care for family and those you leave behind. You can stop drinking. You can stop taking drugs. But with something so elementally a part of the self as sexuality, how can you end the power of its most corrupted form other than by destroying the vessel itself?

The fallout from a full-blown episode can be

devastating. For years any new relationship began under an ominous forecast that at some point the grim faces of those men of my past would appear and demand that whatever love was starting to grow be given back to them.

I was desperate for it to stop, for I had never been offered love like I had that July. I'd been able to silence the compulsion, but I wasn't sure how long could I survive this violence that comes entirely from within. Mia and I walked in the forest one day after a storm, ripped and splintered trees leaving clusters of wooden knives jagged from the soaking earth. We meandered up towards the hill above Loughton, to Great Monk Wood where the largest of the pollards rise, and there we found a swing. It was during that early part of a relationship when everything is so new that you're trying to be positive, all the time. To be cheery and attractive and amusing, as knowledgeable a guide through the woods as you might subsequently be through life.

When we parted at the tube Mia said she wanted me to find her swing again. I wanted that too, but could only see the ropes hanging from the trees like creepers, as if the forest had turned into a jungle. I didn't know if I had become so trapped by the thickets of desire that I wouldn't be able to find a way to make it work with her. I felt so sorry to realise then that I wanted the nylon round my neck more than I wanted to understand the freedom she felt on that swing, pushing her wet hair behind her ears as she asked how to get down.

That's how the forest and depression work hand in hand. Some see the boughs as a challenge – a tree to be climbed and conquered, a thrill to be accessed. But for the suicidal, it looks different. The rope, the tree, the curving beam. Unlike the light fitting to which the man who lived in the forest tried to fix his dog leash, the bough is sturdy and guarantees good purchase, won't rip out plaster and wires and leave you collapsed in a heap on the floor. A tree will take your nylon, your leash, your rope and will make no judgement. It knows that whatever memorials are tied round its branches in Sellotape and ribbon will not survive even one winter. The body will be removed, transported to a place where it might better be disposed of in our embarrassment of death.

The forest suicides know to remove themselves from the city. I suspect they do not want to be found, but this is the only place they have to go. The man who lives in the forest failed in everything he was trying to do. A death wish led him from his village into the forest. He believed that by ceasing the medication that he had thought was the only thing keeping him alive, he would find that offering among a thousand, ten thousand, who knows how many boughs on which to achieve his ending. I never knew how to ask him how his mind, conscious or otherwise, argued this. When I tried to lead our conversations that way, it was as if what I was attempting to say didn't really compute. He had escaped from our convention, the taboo of suicide, the fear of death. As I walked through the dense forest between Theydon and Epping, I looked at every branch and wondered how they called out to him. I wondered at the accident that meant that he stayed alive.

The man in the forest survived – not because he was cut down and rescued by modern science, psychiatry and psychoactive medication, but by disappearing into something so much bigger than himself. His mind was stronger than most. His connection with the forest, and an essential sanity, should not be denigrated or described as madness, for the forest that was to be his ally in death became his saviour. This is not to say that the other suicides of Epping Forest were failures. They found their own peace.

There's a societal awkwardness around suicide, perhaps because of the guilt of friends and relatives that they ought to have noticed something amiss sooner. So many happen out of the blue because someone was good at concealing the chaos. Men account for 75 per cent of suicides in the UK, and men under forty-five are more likely to die by suicide than any other cause. One study by the *Journal of Adolescent Health* found that bisexual youths were more likely to be suicidal than gays or lesbians. Overall, the LGBT suicide rate far outstrips that of the straight community. As the psychiatrist Patrick Carnes revealed in *Out of the Shadows*, his study on the silent and hidden disease of sexual addiction, 17 per cent of addicts have attempted suicide and 72 per cent have considered it.

I have always felt that niggle, looked at the strength of doors and wondered at my height against their frame and the durability of a silk dressing-gown belt or a few metres of fishing line. In my blackest moods in the forest I'd spotted long jumps over the smooth, curved drop of a brook and have surmised that if I were to do it I wouldn't choose one of these places near a path. The secret swing, the special place. Could I find it again? Would I be able to let my feet leave the ground?

In happy periods when I'd been able to stop the ghostly hands of those men manipulating me, the thought that the only way to silence their instructions was to destroy myself seemed faintly ludicrous. But merely a hair trigger could send me back down there, where the idea of forest bathing for a lightening of mood was preposterous, and drowning in the forest, itself a suicide pool of the blackest water on the shores of the city, made perfect sense.

Compulsion is the most exhausting feeling I have ever known, provider of the worst comedown, the grimmest hangovers because they cannot be shared. And the deeper in you go, the more alone you become. There is only one true solution to that utter isolation. As Carnes writes, 'To preserve his integrity, Dr Jekyll has to kill Mr Hyde.'

A few weeks after that first trip to the forest with Mia we walked as part of a big group to a Loughton boozer I'd not been to before, full of the modern south-west Essex sort. They called us 'students', and people drove ostentatious cars slowly past the crowd. I got drunk, too drunk, and felt that familiar, sinking isolation – from her, from my friends. The light was too bright, the air suffocating, it was too loud and words of conversation just would not come. I had to escape.

I went for a piss and slipped out of the pub, hopped the low fence and charged across the road to where street lights picked out the forest opposite in a sickly grey that turned to black as the slope of Staples Hill rose behind it. I shoved my way in over the curb, brambles and nettles attacking my bare legs, the grey arms of street-lit twigs hitting my face, before I found myself right beneath an ancient oak. Alcohol surged through me, and as I breathed deeply in the clammy, mushroomy air I couldn't see my own hand in front of my face, just a glimmer of light through the trees. That vision came back to me then. The figure under the tree of Debden Slade with a noose above his head.

I knew that if I hadn't run and he had raised his head towards me I would have looked into my own eyes. Death by forest or water is a conspiracy with the nature that birthed us and a completion of a cycle. It might be the most natural thing in the world.

16

The Natural Aspect

On the best days of late summer everything is of the sun, as if the light and heat have poured down from the sky to saturate the soil and flood out across the forest.

The cows lazily swished their tails through the rich, warm air as they browsed the fringes of Long Running plain. I saw such a cloud of dragonflies that the air was almost itchy, and they darted in their uptight way above the dowdy flutter of a meadow brown butterfly. The bark of Grimston's Oak was warm to the touch, except on the shaded side where someone had built a shelter against the trunk. All around under the trees at the edges of the clearings were fungi, flashes of red, rich-brown and white where careless foragers had lifted and discarded them. The abundance of the season was such that there were more blackberries than the pickers could cope with, laden crab-apple branches swung heavily in the low wind and sloes awaited the distant frost that would make them right for gin.

A fallow doe thundered across the path, pursued

by a small, yappy dog and its irate owner. I had a chuckle. For the first time in ages I felt contented in the forest. Gradually the ooze of winter's misery was starting to evaporate. Mia had held me in such peaceful understanding that I had started to lower the barriers I instinctively put up to love. I sat against a tree to read a book advising young men on how to satisfy their decadent whims in the sexism and smoke of swinging 1960s London. It was an oddly bleak read and I nodded off, to be woken by the low moo of one of the Corporation's longhorn cows right in front of my face.

Two weeks later, the same paths, the same routes, yet the forest was unrecognisable. For all Mia's patience she was understandably struggling to deal with my volatile moods, my ability at one moment to be overwhelmed by the sweetest intimacy but the next to vanish into a private void as if, she said, I had been taken away. She was as good at delivering short, sharp truths as she was at being understanding. It was exactly what I needed. Yet nobody enjoys being told what they should do. Perhaps I was more like those conventional blokes I'd always loathed than I had thought.

The forest was humid and heavy, the air no longer sweet to drink. It'd rained earlier that day and towering clouds the colour of granite loomed to the north and south, as if the Epping ridge had pushed up to disperse them. Just where I entered the woods a flock of long-tailed tits had made an old oak their temporary home and filled the air with their shrill, caustic tweeting. Where the end of pollarding had closed the canopy and shut out the light the ground was devoid of flora; the fungi had rotted and were now scattered about, black as coal. Squirrels chutt-chutted their irritation, but aside from the heavy rattling of the raindrops they dislodged, the deeper forest was silent. It had an intense weariness, and I could feel the immense weight of all the leaves, ready for the chlorophyll to sink back into the wood before their flaming death. In the few places where light did break through there were no heaven-sent shafts of gold, but harsh spots of brightness on the matt of so many years of leaf-fall. An oak stump broken and craggy as a volcanic outcrop – oak stumps can take a century to finally rot away – glowed a sickly blue.

Late summer is a more ominous, monotonous time even than the depths of winter, when at least the brief hours of light show the forest in a steely contrast and twigs hold the tiny buds that promise spring. August is the silent suffocation. It is in part a consequence of what happened after the forest was saved in 1878. The Corporation was required to preserve its 'natural aspect' and 'protect the timber and other trees, pollards, shrubs, underwood, heather, gorse, turf, and herbage growing on the Forest'. Yet the Conservators responsible for executing this deferred to the Enlightenment view that a forest, in its 'natural' state, consisted of tall trees rising towards the sky. They began a programme of thinning the forest by removing what the nineteenth-century naturalist Alfred Russel Wallace described as 'a hideous assemblage of stunted mop-like pollards'. The ecosystems of the managed landscape, stretching back into the prehistoric mists of memory and time, were suddenly disrupted. With no lopping, the limbs of the pollards grew ever taller and into thick trunks. The beeches raised a new, dense canopy high above, shutting out the sun from the forest floor, suppressing light-reliant plants. The forest started, in the modern buzzword of back-to-nature ecology, to 'rewild' itself. Holly, once a rare species in the forest, benefited from its tolerance of shade and started to fill out the underwood. With grazing much reduced, scrub began to encroach onto the plains and glades, as did light-hungry birch; areas that would once have been open and covered in heather are now home to a tall, swaying army of those grey, papery-trunked trees. Where there are beech pollards they have grown up far more powerfully than their rivals, their crowns excluding all but 3 per cent of sunlight from above, making it nigh on impossible for the flora below to survive. Now that the forest has increasingly gone back to 'nature', free from human interference, it has become a close, intimidating place.

Often when I walked I would have the words of Werner Herzog running on a loop in my head. I'd always admired the German director for his frank engagement with the natural world in his work, and how creating it was frequently an epic struggle against the absolute power of wilderness. I'd found a clip on YouTube, taken from *My Best Fiend*, his account of working with the actor Klaus Kinski on films including *Fitzcarraldo*. The moustachioed director stands in front of thick green leaves. 'I see jungle as being full of obscenity. Nature here is vile and base,' he says, as the camera cuts to footage of a man slicing the wing off a parrot. 'I wouldn't see anything erotical here. I would see fornication and asphyxiation and choking and fighting for survival and growing and then just rotting away.' A bird begins to shriek in uncanny rhythm somewhere off camera. Herzog's words and that pulsing scream would be in my head as I'd walk past the bloodied pile of feathers along the ride, or hornets emerging menacingly from a tree trunk, or step into a bog, fetid ooze overtopping my boot. I'd swear, and the Herzog in my head would continue: 'The trees here are in misery. The birds are in misery. I don't think they sing. They just screech in pain. Taking a close look at what's around us there is a kind of harmony. It is the harmony of overwhelming and collective murder.'

Epping Forest is not the jungle, but on so many of the days that I have walked through it the croak of its jays might indeed signal despair, the trill of those long-tailed tits be as aggravating as tinnitus. The jungle is a cipher for all nature – even damp England in a certain fading light.

Over the past six months I had wanted the forest to do something for me. As a child I had grown up with the belief that in each bright flash of a bud breaking through in spring we might see the entirety of the wonder of God's creation. As an adult society had told me that 'nature' was the place you go when broken-hearted or at a low ebb to be cleansed and healed. None of this had worked on the hundreds of miles I'd stomped through the woodland, my head immune to any of the supposed beauty that was around me but instead cleaved to a fast-blinking reel of hardcore eroticism and self-loathing. The forest didn't care. The moors hadn't cared. I might as well get down on my knees and suck all the men I could find at Eagle Pond, for nature wouldn't care. Nature wouldn't tell anyone, would keep my secrets even if they might end up destroying me. If I died in shame at my own hand afterwards I would just rot down into the soil. Nature would not blink.

I felt exhausted by the mental effort of trying to manage my sexuality into an ecosystem that might be strong enough to resist becoming choked by compulsion and doubt. I was impatient with the increasing awareness that it was not going to be an easy or fast process. Whenever I strived for intimacy in this new love that offered so much, the eyes of those men were always there, their voices muttering that it was not enough.

Now, in my mid-thirties, when everyone around me was doing all the normal things that fixed their place in the city – buying houses, settling down, having children – I could not envisage any of that as part of my future. I'd reacted against what I saw as heteronormative straitjackets because I couldn't see how bisexuality fitted into them. I wanted to be sure in my fluidity, but always felt that I would be denied it as soon as I picked monogamy with one or the other gender. Perhaps this is where the view that bisexuals are sexually voracious stems from. We are forced into non-monogamous sexuality merely to hold on to the ownership of our desires. Sexual compulsion only made this internal split more acute, for it always offered an easy way out, ever the victor in the trial between mind and body.

For a long while I had held on to a line in a song a friend had written about the body renewing itself every seven years, believing that in the passing of time the skin that had been touched would no longer be there; the memories would fade away and I would be able to be and love just like anyone else. In reality it was as if those old acid hands had burned into my body and the wounds were, like the scars on a pollard, becoming more grotesque as I aged.

Our mental-health services are woefully underinvested; only those in acute distress are catered for, and even then inadequately. For those whose minds straddle the edges of the wilderness, functioning depressives or those of us who suffer from anxiety, and especially those who have problems around sexuality, there's little help on offer. I had tried cognitive behaviour therapy, free on the NHS. After I got off the phone to book the first appointment I broke down in tears, relieved that finally I might get some help.

It was a pain to get to the appointment, miles away along one of the neglected lines of the London Overground. The health centre was clearly once a pleasant country house that must have been on the edge of Epping Forest but was now institutional, with all the usual smells of over-zealous cleaning and plants that themselves looked in need of therapy lurking in the corner. The rooms were poky and always too hot.

I knew I was lucky to get the appointment, but I had a sinking feeling as soon as the therapist handed me her pieces of paper. 'Have you been feeling anxious in the last seven days?' *Of course I fucking have that's why I am here.* There were childlike pictures of figures with simplistic questions, flow charts of worry. The first thing I told her was that there were things from my past that I needed to talk about. The first thing she told me was that the past was precisely what we didn't discuss.

Friends recommended mindfulness apps but they didn't work for me either. The gentleness of the American voice, probably a hippy, telling me to feel all the extremities of the body I loathed, telling me that at the end of his ten minutes of waffle I was 'back in the room.' *A room I had never fucking left.* If anything, those quiet, meditative times were the worst, the focus on the irritatingly calm voice merely allowing the hatred and twisted dread inside me to come pouring forth.

With everything else failing, in desperation I knew that I had to go and see the man in the forest. It'd been a few months since my last trip, when he'd materialised in the dusk and confused me with one of his spirits. I called my aunty, who said that his arthritis had worsened and he was no longer able to walk the distance from his camp down the road past their house, and took a bus instead. She suggested I go on a Wednesday, to try and intercept him on his rounds of local friends. The Costa machine in Tesco had always been his connection to the rest of us back in the civilised world, a sort of teleportation device. It seemed as good a place to start as any. Paying for my black Americano, I mentioned the man in the forest by his name and asked the cashier if he'd been in that morning. She looked at me blankly. 'You know,' I said, 'the man with the white hair and the beard. He . . . he lives in a bush in the forest and comes here to buy coffee?' She looked at me as if I were mad.

I took my brew to a bench and sat staring at the line of trees that marched across the tidy village green, as formal as if they were troops press-ganged from the irregular forces in the forest and made to drill. The smart cars of south-west Essex whooshed between them. I could see no sign of the man from the forest. I hadn't realised quite how much I'd missed him. I'd made him some flapjacks and ate one as a phalanx of dog-walkers crossed the green. I supposed they were all about his age, white hair and sensible jackets, little furry balls of tamed wildness on the ends of their leads.

I walked around the green and along the avenue. It was warmer and humid under the oaks, where a man collected fragments of a glass bottle left there by some idiot. By the village pond a woman grinned at me, exposing teeth as brown as the muddy banks. 'You look so happy,' she said, 'it's so nice to see someone smile like that. Will you come home with me?' I told her not now, but didn't explain that the smile was only because the sun was shining and I was squinting as I desperately scanned the green in search of him.

Just as I was starting to worry I'd missed him, a bus came into view from Piercing Hill. There was his familiar silhouette, almost regal, through the window grimed by forest roads. My heart leaped and I ran towards the stop. A woman got off with a load of shopping and a kid, then another with a pram. Then one crutch poked through the bus door, followed by a second, and he laboriously swung himself onto the pavement. 'Haha!'

he shouted, 'Sorry I'm late.' He looked better than when I'd last seen him, the skin on his face and legs the colour of a cup of tea you'd not send back. All that was different was his pace, slowly inching down the pavement on his crutches – 'my racing sticks' he told me as we set off past the Tikadi Hair Salon and Indian Ocean curry house.

He settled into his patter as if we'd never been apart, telling me of a new watch he'd bought in Harlow for twenty-five quid, the tills in WH Smith breaking in his presence – 'she said, "You've put a bloody hex on this." As soon as I walked in the shop both tills fucked up and they wouldn't work.' The traffic stopped as he abruptly swung himself into the road. We made our way across to the village green and the monologue continued unabated. 'The other day I was crossing here where I shouldn't do, there's a van it's got to be a white-van driver innit, well you ought to hear the filth. The filth! He's behind there and he's mouthing off shocking. I said, "That's rude!" and I blew him a kiss, I bloody well did. A young lady that knew me was there and she knows my legs don't work so well but I think she's about a Fourth Dan. I'm protected by ladies!' 'Do the ladies tend to look after you more than the men?' I asked. 'They do. The men, well they think, "You've had a few mild winters, wait till it gets really cold." Not that they'd know, but I've done all that, I've been tested as a young soldier haven't I? Some of those males they're fucking spiteful, going "You fucking dosser."' Worst of all were the golfers whose benches he liked to rest his tired legs on. 'They said, "We don't like this tramp here." Well that's nice! Tramp?! I'm a nemophilist forest dweller! I just told them to fuck off.' The golfers had claimed that he was wandering around in the nude, and apparently had complained to the forest authorities.

He told me about the lavender oil his friend Angela gave him for his joints, Christine's anti-inflammatory pills and a new, more efficient way of eating his meals by simultaneously squirting tomato puree and American-mustard mayonnaise directly into his mouth. His social life had been keeping up too, including an invite to one of the houses on the old Copped Hall estate to see an eagle. He critiqued the paintings by local artists in the window of the shop and seemed chuffed that my uncle had painted his portrait, sat on a bench and feeding the birds.

My phone rang – my aunty asking when I was going to be round for lunch. I thought of the forest hermits of yore and how young men and women would go to them for advice, something I'd not yet done with the man who lives in the forest, preferring to hear his stories and listen to the forest speak through him.

My own depression had taught me that the slightest thing could trigger a return to twisted places, and that was the last thing I wanted for him. But when I asked, 'How have you been, really been?' he replied without hesitating. 'I tell you what, do you know what it's been splendid, splendid, splendid,' he said. 'It's been the happiest three years of my life, the best three years. My guardian angels, my spirits, they must be looking out for me. I don't do bloody recession, bloody manic depression any more, like I haven't been since I've been in the forest.'

He was such a talker that I hadn't much mentioned myself in any of our other meetings, and he wasn't really the sort to ask. But as my pocket buzzed with another call I felt a sudden panic that I might not see him again, that he might fade into the forest just as swiftly and strangely as he had appeared in my life. I blurted out that I wasn't feeling at all well and didn't know what to do.

He turned to look at me with eyes that burst from his white bushy squint in an explosion of blue. He paused before he said, as if there were no other advice he could have given, 'Well maybe you should just plonk yourself down in the forest for a while.'

17

Flesh and Wood

As the Central Line clattered back down towards central London I looked out at the flashes of forest between suburbia and felt perplexed. This was ridiculous. There was no way I could just plonk myself down in the forest next to my wizened old friend.

The doors opened at Stratford and I got out to the din of people running between train lines and the Westfield shopping mall. Shoves. Shouts. It was the evening rush hour and I stood on the Overground squished into the silent carriage next to a fashion student loudly bitching into her mobile. Never mind the man who lives in the forest's holly-bush home, *this* wasn't for me either.

It was hard to convey my muddled sensibility to others. I quacked on about the forest to so many people, covered my Instagram feed with pictures of it, and was asked to find locations for picnics, walks, pubs, blackberry-picking, sloe-collecting for gin, the best spots for wild garlic or to see a deer, how to camp overnight and get away with it, the best place to trip on magic mushrooms without risk of an excess of psychic disturbance. People must have assumed it to be a dearly beloved place for me, rather than one that was conflicted and twisted and strange. If they came back from their visits feeling refreshed and ready to face whatever the world might chuck at them it was because they didn't have the same expectation of the forest that I did. I'd reached a level of obsession with the place which had become unhealthy. The man who lived in the forest had left civilisation and gone into nature and it had absolutely saved his life. But it was not my solution.

I needed to find a way to break these demands that I kept enforcing on the forest, on myself. It wasn't just those words of Werner Herzog, listened to on repeat via YouTube, that showed me that there were other ways of approaching the forest that might be more rewarding than the mass sigh of 'Ah, nature' that I'd found so frustrating and that didn't work for me. If I could see in the forest the grey areas and complexities I saw within myself, perhaps then I could find a place of constantly renegotiated equilibrium within it, or at least an acceptance that we are forever in a similar state of flux. If nothing in Epping Forest is natural, then neither is there a correct way to behave within it.

Herzog is right – there is no morality to nature. It just *is*, and we may do what we will within it, as constituent elements. In his 1959 visionary exploration of memory and locality *Poetics of Space*, Gaston Bachelard quotes René Ménard as saying, 'In the forest, I am my entire self. Everything is possible in my heart just as it is in the hiding places in ravines. Thickly wooded distance separates me from moral codes and cities.'

Epping Forest has no rules aside from those which were imposed upon it in the form of by-laws, marked up on boards around the car parks. Yet more powerful even than these are the unspoken societal codes as to what constitutes appropriate behaviour within nature. The idealised view of it often has at its heart a desire to push away other people. It's claimed that this is for the good of the hillside, forest or so on, but really it seems it's for the good of the individual. It's often as if, in a beautiful place, you're in a queue of others waiting for you to get out of the way so they might take a picture or gain maximum edification. I'd no doubt been guilty of it myself. And some of our most fetishised natural locations are being destroyed by our excessive love of them, from the erosion of the Lakeland hills to Thoreau's Walden Pond, now polluted by phosphates from nature pilgrims urinating in it.

I'd always been conscious walking through the forest of the negative impacts of human activity – the fly-tipped mounds of bin bags and building waste in car parks, the delicate forest floor sliced by the tyres of off-road cyclists. More troubling was the ever-present question of what would happen to the forest in this era of dramatic climate change. It was clear that humans all too often spoil and destroy habitats in Epping Forest just as much as they do anywhere else in the world. Yet the more I looked into Epping Forest's history, the more I came to understand that it owed its existence almost entirely to the work of human hands. Held within this complexity was a truth that went beyond the nature-versus-human dynamic. It was all-encompassing, embracing them both and all of us, including me.

The rewilding of the forest after the end of regular management didn't coincide with a return to seeing it as radical, mystical, erotic. We haven't tried to divine a holistic engagement that might become part of a necessary renegotiation of our relationship with the natural world. Instead, the passive process of walking, cycling or strolling is as selfish an exchange as logging. It demands of the forest that we acquire our respite, solace or physical refreshment without offering any deeper philosophical or sensual engagement in return. What do we give back to the forest now, save a film of pollution, picnic detritus and dog turds in plastic bags?

The Epping Forest archives offered up a sensational array of human stories that had played out under its cover in the century and a bit since it was protected for the betterment of the people of London. These citizens hadn't done what they were supposed to, and used nature to cleanse the dirt from our supposedly modern minds. Epping Forest was saved for the people of London, but London couldn't help but keep breaking through, disrupting nature, with its human instinct for dirt, vice, volume.

I loved those musty old articles in the blue folders in the London Metropolitan Archives, not least because they were often hilarious and cheered me up, their highfalutin Victoriana and atmosphere of moral panic palpable in the yellowed paper. As the summer went on I committed more and more of them to memory, and each time I walked through the forest I would enjoy imagining the ribald scenes playing out amid the trees.

The appearance of so many Londoners in the forest had caused consternation among locals in what had previously been a fairly remote and rural area. In June 1875 the *East London Observer* complained that visitors 'enjoy the scenery less than the mild ale or other strong potions available in the local inns, while some of them make night and day hideous in their going and returning'. Children from the East End were taken to the forest for health and improvement, but they'd be followed by locals with water carts, washing the streets behind them. The Victorian popular press devoted column inches to the nightmare of 'rowdyism', printing vicious tirades against working-class visitors to the forest. Much of this was a reaction to the physicality of the people, their perceived baseness, their dirty bodies and minds corrupted, supposedly, by poverty and sin. There was the thinly disguised anxiety that the assembled multitudes of East Enders were a strong gin or a bawdy song away from disappearing into the woods to fuck. It wasn't dissimilar to the Christian morality that had so terrified me in those years of confusion about my sexuality – the line between sanctity and damnation seemed a fine one. I saw the great and the good of Victorian masculinity down in the Corporation, with their stovepipe hats and sideburns, as the elders of some strict religious sect, imposing rules on the forest, and the all-male keepers as their priestly enforcers.

They gendered the forest, trying to do away with its potential for sexual disruption by equating it with innocence and purity, and any interference with it as a defilement. The untouched forests of distant lands were described as 'virgin'. The notion that the forest is somehow sexually innocent or pure can even be seen in the way in which a tree that hasn't been pollarded or coppiced is referred to as a 'maiden' tree, just as for a woman to lose her virginity was once described as the taking of her maidenhood. When in 1896 the *Daily News* decried the 'most revolting scene' of the Easter Fair, it used the image of the city violating the feminised ideal of nature: 'Is it really worthwhile for the Corporation of London to allow another great fair to be growing up on the skirts of their splendid great forest?' Within these diatribes there lurked squeamishness at the sensuality of the forest and a desire to control it with patrician morality.

What had been done there over the centuries was ambiguous and varied. The forest and newspaper archives tell of riots, unlicensed preaching, political agitation, robbery, drunkenness, illegal gherkin sellers, poaching, blinding songbirds to use as decoys to attract and then cage more, gambling, prog-rock concerts, female boxing, children trampled by a donkey derby gone out of control, dogging, wiccan rituals, biker meets, an unnatural act with a sheep near Debden, poaching, crazed Aunt Sallies, perverts on bicycles, teenage catapulters of swans, the first motocross race. It was a history as vibrant and wonderful as that of any city in the world.

I discovered that in 1975 Cosey Fanni Tutti of COUM Transmissions and Throbbing Gristle had, twenty years after Genesis P-Orridge attended the same forest-side school as my dad, modelled for a porn magazine shoot up in Epping Forest. The photos, published in volume twelve of *Exposure* magazine under the title 'My Driving Instructress Gave Me a Lesbian Love Lesson in Her Car', capture awkward sex in a cramped space, sunlit trunks of birch trees in the background, a screen of bushes stretching into the distance. It may be pornography, but it looks pretty real. Cosey lives by the maxim, 'My life is my art, my art is my life' and used these images as exhibits in her own artistic practice, subverting the exploitative expectations of pornography, especially that of the time. The forest had become part of sex, part of art, part of life. The place of innocence as defined by those fusty men of the Corporation and simpering poets alike was all too easily subverted. It was something I loved about the forest and its possibilities.

By September that year, the forest had come more alive for me than ever, these hurdy-gurdies and ghostly voices on charabancs gone wild drifting through my imagination. Sometimes the modern world hurtled in to offer up its own stories for documentation. On a Sunday morning walk I was surprised to see quite so many people suddenly emerging from the trees looking perplexedly at their phones. With their saucer eyes and white trainers soiled by the forest, I suspected they might have something to do with the gentle thudding BPM of a sound system in the distance. They'd vanish, then appear again, clearly lost. 'Mate,' a bloke in reflective sunglasses asked me through his gurn, 'where the fuck am I?' It transpired they'd all been at a rave that had thundered on through the night undisturbed, somewhere up near Cuckoo Brook. I looked under the

Epping Forest location tag on Instagram and found pictures of an impressive set-up that would rival any indoor club – they'd up-lit the trees and hung mobiles above the dancefloor clearing. A few days later someone told me that they'd done it right, too, and taken their litter home. I was glad raves were happening in the forest, just as I was glad the cruising ground at Eagle Pond was still popping.

All of this glorious human life is able to carry on underneath the cover of nature. There is no duality, it all just *is*, wood and flesh as co-conspirators against orthodoxies and rules. So long as we take our litter home, we might not do the forest any harm. Equally, it might not do any damage to us. I was hardly about to start pickling gherkins and illegally selling them in the forest, but I was all for a queering of the landscape. In it I could perhaps finally learn not to fear myself.

Gradually I began to dispute the judging voices that I constantly turned against myself. God, society, compulsion, my own long-standing internalisation of bisexual erasure – it was maddening listening to them all at once, and I'd had enough. But the self-confidence I felt in those days was fleeting.

A few weeks after the man who lived in the forest had thrown down the gauntlet by suggesting that I go and become an apprentice forest spirit alongside him, I'd ended up having an unexpected row with my parents about sexuality. It had reopened up the toxic panic that my bisexuality was merely a repressed homosexuality desperate to be unleashed. I'd spent so many years avoiding these conversations, living in a private hinterland of my own making, that having them now seemed to be even more unsettling than they might have been during my teenage years. Yet I still wasn't capable of resenting my parents for the beliefs that they held so dear and, indeed, were starting to change – which was partly why the dispute had been so sharp and unexpected. Nevertheless, I found myself pushed back into a deep anxiety over my complicated desires. I felt entirely dysfunctional in the context of a relationship and once again withdrew. Mia had finally had enough and said she couldn't cope. It was predictable. I was bored with myself.

It was to be a hot week in the capital, with the promise of the warmest September day in decades. As I checked the weather on my phone for the last time before slipping on an eye mask, the symbol of the full sun promised something special and I nodded off into my nightmares with renewed hope.

Far above the first train the next morning airliner contrails threaded through the milky end of night into the heart of the coming sun. The sky was red through ragged grey cloud, like blood beneath a scab as the clock on the platform at Chingford showed it was just a few minutes until sunrise at 6.30 a.m. I pegged it through the barriers and down the familiar stretch of road past the Masons, Flabélos and the driving school, and onto Chingford Plain. Summer was in denial about its end, but the air hinted at the imminent change of season, tasting damp and loaded with the sourness of rotting fruit from the blackberry bushes surrounding the golf-club café. I drank into it deeply, coughing a little through a morning greeting to a dog walker as I overtook him.

Ahead, the grassland was covered by a neck-deep sea of vapour over which the Royal Forest pub and Queen Elizabeth's Hunting Lodge loomed like dockside warehouses. In the far distance the trees in front of the quickening sky were cast into thick shadow above the haze, though the sun was still hidden behind a bank of low cloud. I didn't have a plan, and meandered to and fro.

The mowers had done their work and the wild flowers that had covered the plain were all gone, re-placed by the silvery sparkle of the dew. Up on the slope by Queen Elizabeth's Hunting Lodge a chestnut, always the sentinel of the changing seasons, had already shriv-elled into brown. Small flies bothered me, biting at my legs, and I picked my way down through an archipelago of cowpats past the mostly sleeping cattle of the Epping Forest herd. One raised its horns and snorted with what I could swear was derision. I was quite enjoying myself, pootling around, not really thinking about why I was there or what I was doing. I had given up on the forest offering me any kind of solace, and the absence of the desperate expectations I had dragged through it before was a weight off my shoulders. I felt very alone, but calm.

The break-up hadn't played out as I'd experienced with similar situations in the past, when separation would send me plunging into the excitable prowl in search of the encounters that was my favourite drug. I'd not needed to push us both through such an awful place of loss. The resignation clung to me like the last of the mist drifting over the blackthorn. I stood on the short grass, back to the sun, and watched my shadow lengthen towards the forest until I became a spindly wraith. I swung my arms around, the shadow waved back. I chased it, running towards the forest.

As I skirted the edge of the plain the air tasted unsure of itself, wet and cold on the lips and in the lungs. Warmth billowed out from the treeline, as if the forest had been storing it overnight under its duvet of trees. I dived in and it smelled spiced, almost churchy.

I took deep breaths and zigzagged in and out of the trees and the patches of cold mist as if I were swimming through fresh water.

18

No Dark Secrets

The Grunewald covers 3,000 hectares to the west of Berlin. I can't remember whether I first heard about it from a friend or fly-pasts on Google Maps, but the same voice that told me I needed to get up to catch the 06.12 to Chingford to see the sunrise over the plain insisted that I had to go there. An urge again, just like the one that kept sending me to High Beach after Alice and I had broken up, and had sent me down the Pennine Way to Stoodley Pike. My compulsions extended to whims to visit places as much as they did sex.

I peered past my neighbour in seat 21A of the EasyJet Airbus as we climbed out of Gatwick towards Berlin. I could just glimpse the dull-green arc of Epping Forest in the distance. I wasn't as childishly excited as I usually was when I saw the forest from a plane, just overcome with relief to be getting away from London, from the relationship that I'd again succeeded in shaking to bits and the turmoil of the row I had had with my parents. I needed the distraction.

Berlin is a city that reminds me of London at the turn of the millennium, right down to the style of graffiti in the toilets of the bars that never close, where it's easy to slide into a nocturnal mode of existence. Everyone is mysteriously attractive and interesting-looking and appears to be doing something, even if they achieve very little.

The way London had changed in the intervening decade and a half had an odd effect on my sense of belonging. It was as if the dread deathliness of the Little England I'd grown up in was starting to infiltrate the capital, and like a cancer kill it from within. Although all my Berlin friends would tell me that *their* city wasn't what it was ten or twenty years ago, to me it was a revelation. Much of this was to do with its openness and tolerance of sexuality, and how this deeply intersected with art and music in a way that stuffy, binary Britain could never quite achieve. This was never more apparent than during visits to Berghain, a gigantic nightclub based in a former power station on the border between the old West and East Berlin.

On a Sunday, its busiest day, Berghain more than lives up to its reputation for hedonism, yet I've always found it to be a curiously wholesome, welcoming place. Most of what is written about Berghain goes on about exclusivity and debauchery, but to me it's a beautifully democratic space that feels autonomous and out of step with the real world outside. You're made to hand over your phone on entry so that a small sticker can be placed over the camera. There's such respect for the rules that I've never seen anyone try to take a surreptitious photograph. Once inside – powered by a sound system so clean and heavy that it carries the body – the lack of digital voyeurism is liberating. It is, as was Ian's house, a defiantly queer space where I was entirely at home. Just like the forests, Berghain knows no morality or rules and I've never felt the sting of shame over anything I have done there, in that respectful congregation of desire. It was one of the few places that held my fluid sexuality steady and calm.

At Berghain a few days after I arrived in Berlin I drained three bottles of Club Mate, an energy drink that apparently once had something to do with raisins. As the bass massaged the air I talked to German pals about this forest to the west of their city. I was told that a cycling-obsessed Turkish friend was now afraid to ride far beyond it for fear of being pushed off his bike by thugs emboldened by the resurgence of racism and the far right. Someone wondered if it had been felled in the harsh years following the Second World War, another said that no, it was too far out and only the linden trees of the Tiergarten had gone, sawed to pieces in front of the shattered Reichstag. People were curious about Epping Forest. Full of enthusiasm for its unusual histories, I explained the battle to save it, the artists, the writers, the nutters, the cruisers. But they told me that, unlike my forest, the Grunewald held no dark secrets.

If there really were no dark secrets in the Grunewald, perhaps my own troubles might dissipate through its trees like fog burned away by the dawn. The anxious compulsion to visit the place took hold of me as I stood half-heartedly not quite dancing in front of one of

Berghain's giant speakers. A topless woman leading a man haltered by a collar and chain walked right past me, but I barely noticed as I wondered if my brogues were sturdy enough for a walk the next day.

A few hours later, with a splitting headache from the Club Mate and ruined sleep, I took the U-Bahn and then the S- out past the open space of Tempelhof Airport, clattering through suburbs and fields of quaint summer houses where Berliners spend their weekends. The hot air carried a foul whiff from a giant turd of unknown mammalian origin on one of the seats. Opening windows just seemed to distribute it more evenly around the train. It was a relief to get out at the Nikolassee S-Bahn station and take the bridge over the Autobahn (the Grunewald is crossed by a far larger road than is Epping Forest, though perversely it seems rather clean in comparison, kept away in a concrete trench rather than the litter-and-pollution-fringed rip of the New Road) to where bikers sat drinking next to a huge, glistening café selling Wurst. As cliché demands, they looked a lot more genteel and ordered than the Epping Forest bikers gathered round the green tea hut up at High Beach.

The S-Bahn trip along the edge of the forest had taken a lot longer than I had been expecting, and I realised that to reach the north to find my way back to the centre of the city was going to be a bigger undertaking than I'd planned. Already overheating, I ducked into a service station and bought an extra couple of litres of water and a packet of tiny sausages for the walk ahead. There was one more road to cross, where lorries sat parked up for a takometre break, before I disappeared into the trees and the shade.

Despite the distant sound of the S-Bahn it was calm under the trees. Stands of pine, a species absent from Epping, were scattered among the oak and hornbeam, and gave the air a warm, resinous quality, the hope of secrets in a long-forgotten antique drawer. A walker came in the other direction, casting his eyes about. I kept looking back and saw him stop in front of a tree and start touching it, then his own shoulders, again and again.

Light was hitting me from all sides, flickering against my eyes as if I were in a car driving fast down a long, tree-lined road. Although the Grunewald is made up of very similar species to Epping Forest – hornbeam, oak, silver birch – the atmosphere was entirely different. The trees rose true and straight. My mind started to climb up, the tops far above me swaying at ease against the rich blue sky. The late-summer light filtered through the high canopy to touch the leaf mould and grasses with ruddy flashes and greens, like a carpet of shattered stained glass. The ground was dry and sandy, and beetles with shells glistening like fish scales trotted across as wooden snow drifted down from a wood-pecker hammering high above. The route wound along shallow valleys; at junctions the way was highlighted by white paint on stones. I thought of Epping Forest and how across most of it the view from the rides would be obscured by the thickets of holly and silver birch or young beech. There was something intensely liberating about the lack of congestion here, the gentle breeze and the freedom to walk in any direction without brambles or holly tearing at your legs. I sang to myself as I wandered along, stopping to talk to a big beetle as it pushed a piece of something's shit in one direction, then the other, then another, before giving up and scurrying off the sandy path.

So busy was I marvelling at the beetle's Sisyphean antics that I'd not realised I was almost at my destination, the white domes of the old listening station from where various secret organisations of the NATO alliance had peered into East German territory during the Cold War. It was a steep climb up a wide clearing from the shit-rolling beetle to the top of the hill, where security fencing still surrounded the complex – holes cut in it had been filled, and next to them angry notices warned that the police would prosecute anyone caught entering. My fantasies of pretending I was a Russian agent creeping around the dereliction were disappointed, however, when I eventually stumbled across the main entrance. A woman sat behind a table smoking a joint pointed to a sign announcing a seven-euro fee to enter. I reluctantly paid up, and headed in.

Field Station Berlin Teufelsberg is in a fairly parlous state these days. After the end of the Cold War various groups had put forward plans to turn it into a spy museum, flats or a luxury hotel – at one point David Lynch considered setting up a transcendental meditation centre there. Now the panels on the geodesic domes that once covered the listening equipment have started to break and fray, and most of the buildings are covered in terrible graffiti, 'fuck capitalism' scrawls, cartoon characters, zombies, cyber punks, monsters, the Guy Fawkes mask that came to symbolise the Occupy movement – a garish compendium of pot-addled crusty-culture cliché. Every time I found an open door and tried to wander inside a building I'd get caught by a hippy who'd angrily shoo me out.

Irritated, I stomped back out through the gate and went to look for the lake that Google Maps told me was in the shadow of the hill, stopping to sit on a bench and scoff a few mini sausages as I stared at the view of the treetops that covered the way I'd come, right off into the far distance. As I chewed on the cheap pork meat I noticed something odd. All around the bench, and then I realised further into the undergrowth, were bricks, lumps of concrete and other building materials. I assumed they must be from some now demolished part of the Field Station, but as I walked down the slope I discovered more and more, some cut stone as if from the faces of buildings, roof tiles, bricks still fixed together in clumps, twisted metal. They weren't just by the wayside either, clearly not material brought up here to construct rights of way like the crushed brick that's used to reinforce the rides of Epping Forest.

My shoes were dusty, my shirt grubby with sweat and the fine-blown dust of the path and scrapes from trying to break into the Field Station. Aside from my irritation with the hippies, the walk and the light under the trees had done something to me that Epping Forest had failed to, gently evaporating the truculent miasma of stress and anxiety that I had carried between myself and loved ones for months. I thought of how I had managed to get through the time since Mia had put a hold on things without rushing headlong into the quest for anonymous sex. I missed her too much for that.

Looking out across these long views between tall, straight trunks, it was if I could see how the neglected pollards and density of the forest I was obsessed with back home might have been intensifying whatever negative sensibility I brought into it. I'd taken too much of myself into the forest during a terrible time, and had expected too much of it in return. Here I felt a way out, and as I stopped to plug my phone into a battery pack to make sure I had enough charge to find the Teufelsee lake, I almost chuckled, as if happiness had been catching up with me, and tripped over my toes when I paused.

I didn't need the map to find the Teufelsee; shouts and laughter leaked through the trees with the odd splash, and I walked towards them. Germans seem to like to shit indiscriminately in the woods, and the area was littered with pieces of toilet roll. It was a lot grottier than the spunky discards of the Epping Forest cruising ground, and it stank. One hollowed-out trunk seemed to have been co-opted as a portaloo, and I had to take a wide berth from the fetid latrine, buzzing with flies. Quite who would want to squat in such a confined space where others have squatted before was beyond me.

A waft of fresh air soothed my offended nose and the lake appeared through the trunks, the sudden flash of the surface throwing the thick foliage on the other side of the water in sharp relief. Along the grassy bank people sat on their towels, drinking beer, smoking, chatting, reading.

It was all very civilised. And they were mostly very naked. Like many who were teenagers during the 1990s, I'd acquired the idea that Germans take their clothes off at any opportunity from the late-night TV show *Eurotrash*. In a pre-internet age, it offered the promise of bare flesh accompanied by the ludicrously exaggerated French accents of presenters Antoine de Caunes and fashion designer Jean Paul Gaultier. In every episode, alongside the Swedish swingers, Italians with pendulous breasts, Belgians who liked to dress as penguins and sundry eccentrics whose translated voiceovers were done in regional British accents, there was always a moment when de Caunes would announce, 'An' now, zee ne-kad Jeerrmans!' Even then it struck me as proof that our Continental friends were far more at ease with their bodies than us uptight, neurotic Brits. However much the main interest in watching *Eurotrash* was mild titillation, 'zee ne-kad Jeerrmans' felt rather quaint.

The popularity of naturism in Germany has its roots in health and youth movements of the late nineteenth century. Until the Nazis clamped down on the practice during their twelve years of terror, the act of removing one's clothes and lying around in the natural world was seen as a socially radical act that might lead towards a utopian, egalitarian society. Journals were published, and naturist clubs sprang up across the country. There was even a school of nudity intended to promote healthy relations between the sexes, where the first International Congress on Nudity was held in 1929. After the Second World War the Communist leadership in the East relaxed the Nazis' edicts, seeing nudism as an important element of left-wing thought.

The man who lives in the forest liked to sunbathe nude on the hillside above Copped Hall by the M25, and had told me about a Dutch woman and Turkish man who'd once joined him for an afternoon of worship to his favourite deity, the sun goddess Arethusa. He of course told me that it was 'lovely, just lovely', and that the dog-walking ladies of Epping would call out across the long grass to check that he was 'decent' before coming to say hello. His one-man crusade to make Epping Forest an unofficial nudist colony sadly came to an end when a more conservative local made a complaint, and he was handed a caution. I doubt he was aware that he was continuing a proud local tradition: Essex was once home to radical communes that, just as in Germany, espoused naturism as part of a wholesome and egalitarian life. But that's all gone now. Across England, our nudist beaches are at best hidden away behind mountains of gravel like in Brighton, or increasingly policed and shut down thanks to the never-ending paedo-panic that is a tabloid-inspired national hobby.

An ex-girlfriend of mine, born to hippy parents in California, had introduced me to naturism on trips to hot springs in the north of the state. As someone who since the weekly terror of PE lessons had developed an intense bodily disgust that resulted in a period of near-anorexia, I'd found the experience of wandering starkers around the hot pools of Harbin Springs liberating. Stripping the human body of clothes also stripped it of sexual connotations. It chipped away at my inherited English prudishness, and its close cousin prurience.

As I took off my clothes and plonked my belongings down on the grass, a gentle breeze tickled my skin. The light that had been thrown over my thoughts during the long walk from the south had reached full luminosity. With everything tally-whacking around, I strode down to the water, waded through the mud, and plunged into the Teufelsee.

You can tell a lot about a society by how it likes to swim, and where. In London the municipal pools of the Victorian and Edwardian eras were pleasant, ordered places, created like the saving of Epping Forest out of a patrician philosophy of improvement and concern. The modern pool down near my office in King's Cross, on the other hand, felt like a sop to the local council from the developers, who were transforming the area. Things were frequently broken, the pool was shallow, the ceiling low, the water sour with chlorine. It was like swimming in bleach compared to this.

I wondered how such a lovely spot had come to be called the Teufelsee – the Devil's Lake – and if it had once harboured the connotations of the 'suicide pool'. Those thoughts didn't last, however. The water tasted brackish and refreshing. Flipping over onto my back and gently sculling along, I saw my skin glowing through the greeny-blue-brown down into the depths below, and looked across the undulating surface of the water to the trees and the sky beyond. The sharp differences in temperature as I moved around the lake reminded me of those I'd wandered through in Epping Forest's dawn a few weeks before, but this time my mind was massaged by a contentment I'd not felt in months.

Refreshed and dripping, I picked my way through the bodies scattered across the green. It was cleansing. It was right. It was a place where, like Berghain a few kilometres away, I could feel absolutely at home. No staring, no awkwardness, no shame, just hundreds of bodies, all crinkles and wrinkles, much like the Epping Forest pollards – a woman with a giant arse like a jelly popped from a mould, men's buttocks collapsed and hairy, cocks from the size of my service-station sausage snacks to a couple thick as branches. I felt comfortable in my male form without needing the affirmation of another. If I could do this every weekend, then surely my neuroses and doubts might be washed away by the water, by the light, by this wholesome German forest air.

But then I felt the eyes. If at some point in life you've been sexual prey, you acquire a sixth sense about suddenly becoming an object of interest. I stood above my bag, trying to dry myself a little with my shirt, and surreptitiously looked around, using the flapping cotton as cover.

He wasn't hard to spot. In fact, I was surprised I hadn't noticed him before. My eyes had clearly tried to avoid registering this perfect human stretched out naked in front of me, a shaved head and long neck curving down the smooth skin of his back to a bum so pert it almost vibrated. A rushing sensation caused me to swoon and I wobbled. The lake disappeared and the people too, the tingle of virtuous exercise pushed aside by a far more intense and familiar feeling, at once comforting and dangerous.

I knew he was staring at me as I sat drying in the sun. I could feel his eyes wandering over my skin, as if they were fingers and he was already touching me. I couldn't resist letting my eyes kiss his. They were hazel and deep and warm as the water. He laughed, and I smiled back. He shifted, deliberately pushing his bum into the air as he uncoiled himself from the towel, a tall, sinewy body. His hips swung and as he approached me his semi-hard cock quivered in the sun.

He offered me a cigarette and lay down. 'You're English,' he responded in surprise when I said 'Hello'. Englishmen are apparently not often found naked at the Devil's Lake. I laughed and said I was surprised to find a South African here among the naked Germans of the Grunewald. He told me he'd watched me strip. He'd watched me swim, and he'd watched me return up the bank. He told me that last night he'd been at a party and had drunk too much, and had jumped in his car to drive here from the city to deal with his hangover with water and sun. He told me what he wanted me to do to him, and that I should follow him into the trees. He rose, hand over crotch not hiding much, and walked up the slope.

I stood up and followed him without really being aware I was doing so, as if the waters of the lake had suddenly overflowed their banks and were washing me up after him towards the forest. I walked half stumbling as quickly as I could after his gracefully moving form, my eyes fixed on the gentle undulations of his bum with each stride up over the short grass, the skin of his back rippling like the water of the lake. I moved as quickly as I could lest the rushing adrenaline and blood give me away to the middle-aged couple absorbed in *Der Bild* to my right.

That familiar gale began once again, driving my body forwards into the forest. His form moving hypnotically through the tree trunks called me in closer, his angel buttocks shivering into his thighs, the occasional glimpse of his cock as he slyly turned to see if I was following.

Of course I was. I had no choice. The rest of the world had disappeared and it was as if we had travelled through time, the two of us naked and hard in a small clearing. Just as he reached out for me and I for him, I felt the intense wave rush back, my hot face suddenly cooled, the fug of desire that had led me to this place, that had led me to these places since I was fourteen, dissipated. I heard a voice in the back of my head, the voice of a person I had been trying so hard to love.

Mia had heard something I'd once said – 'Epping Forest can be whatever utopia you want it to be so long as you take your litter home' – and told me that it was about me, that the forest, any forest, might become a complicated place if you take the litter of the mind in with you and are unable to dispose of it there.

I stepped back. He did too. He looked around and said perhaps we were too close to people. There was shit everywhere after all. The moment vanished with our hard-ons. We walked back different ways to the slope by the lake, and when we sat down again he handed me a piece of paper with his telephone number and his name and said I should call later so I could fuck him in my hotel room. I put my shorts back on and the number in my pocket and said I might, and walked off. His note went into the first bin I found.

There's always a regret at not surrendering, and my mind played out a hallucinatory pornographic rendering of what might have happened, the feeling of the skin of his chest tightening under my tongue, looking up as the tips of my fingers traced the shadows on his chest and his brown eyes gazed down at me from the fractured kaleidoscope of the leaves above. But I had been led by my heart this time, and knew it was better left as a fiction.

Perhaps it was guilt, but of a different kind; the shame that had long stalked my sexuality had, recently and all too late in life, started to fade. It felt different from the Monday afternoon behind Eagle Pond, when those who had beckoned me to join them had been ugly to the extent that I'd not have given them the time of day had I met them in a club. There in the Grunewald I would have felt no qualms about disappearing and entwining myself with a man who looked like so many of those who had populated years of fantasies, were it not for another emotion intervening. This had everything to do with a new love that I had thought might already be over but so clearly wasn't, and a voice that called to me to swing with her beneath the trees.

Trying to collect myself, I sat down under a tree and Googled the Grunewald. The Teufelsberg, it told me, meant Devil's Mountain and was named after the adjacent lake, but it was not a natural mountain at all. At the end of the Second World War much of Berlin had been reduced to rubble by years of British and American air raids and the brutality of the Red Army's advance into the city. It all had to be cleared before reconstruction could begin. The Nazis had been building a military technical college out in the Grunewald, to the west of the city and just south of the monumental Olympic stadium. Designed by Albert Speer, it occupied a site on the edge of the forest that had once been a neighbourhood of thousands of homes, many of them belonging to Jews. Adolf Hitler himself had laid the first foundation stone for the Faculty of Defence Technology on 27 November 1937, but the war stopped construction after little more than basement bunkers had been completed. The post-war authorities decided it would make an ideal dumping ground for the ruins of the capital of the thousand-year Reich. From Grunewald Station the Nazis had deported thousands of Berlin's Jews and homosexuals to their deaths in the concentration camps of Theresienstadt and Auschwitz. After the war, those same railway tracks carried the detritus of the violence that the Nazi regime had brought upon its own capital. Seventy-five million cubic metres of the blasted city were transported to the Grunewald, the walls and roofs, bricks and beams of what were once shops, homes, offices, bars, churches. No doubt crushed among the trillions of fragments were some of the men, women and children who died under the onslaught. The piling went on for two decades, the page I read on my phone told me, until the new hill rose 120 metres above sea level. In old photos the dirt looks bright amid the surrounding forest, the tallest thing in the landscape for miles around, but it hadn't taken long for the Grunewald to reclaim the slopes and this unintended memorial to hundreds of thousands of dead as its own, to make appear natural something that had never been.

A text arrived, calling me back to the city. I jumped up and dusted myself off, feeling calmer and more certain that I had done the right thing. The light that evening was as perfect an orange as I'd seen all summer, beams piercing the trees like spotlights picking out patches of the forest floor as if awaiting actors. From the edge of the Teufelsberg I walked with arms outstretched, just as in that Epping dawn a crucifix shadow cast far ahead of me along the sandy path burnished a searing gold in the last flare of the sun.

19

The Last Walk

The weekend after I returned home from Berlin I went to KAOS, a queer techno nightclub that was one of the last places in London that offered some of the same freedom as the German capital. My friend DJ'd, conjuring a room full of people dressed in black (if they had many clothes on at all) into dancing.

Alice was there too. On other occasions, when we'd both been at the same gig or gathering in the pub, I'd envied those who, after a relationship ends, deal with seeing an ex by making a terrible scene. At least they had an outlet. Instead I bottled it all up. Who wants to look like the possessive fool who cannot let go? The masochism that takes hold after a break-up dictates the assumption that your other half is doing better than you are as you wallow. Those things we found irritating are once again endearing; their physical being, now it is out of reach, becomes a stranger who haunts an eroticised realm. Their new lives and loves must be better than the one they left with you.

It's harder to escape the taunts of a broken relationship now, when the digital age requires that we put in considerable effort to avoid setting traps for ourselves. Alice and I had done all the sensible things – unfollowing each other on social media – but every time I'd looked at a Facebook event I'd been planning to go to and seen her face peering out of the list of those attending, I felt anxiety twist into my gut. There was one gig we both went to where the pain of the break-up had been so fresh that it felt wrong that we were now two entirely separate lives temporarily orbiting within the same space. It was made maddening by the hectic music blasting out from the stage. It didn't help that she looked incredible that night, and every time she laughed I was taken back to those uncountable laughs we'd shared together, and heard them all again, at once. I'd had to leave, and again went home convulsed by regret.

There was something deeper too about that sadness, the reason why I still held on. It was clear that the violent swirls of sexual compulsion were what had eventually done for that relationship and so many more. They were what had made me withdraw, whispering to me of the liberated possibilities of non-monogamous single life. But it had all been a false promise. What we'd shared had been more magical than any of those fleeting moments, those fantastical scenarios of debauched imagination. Every time I saw her I was reminded that I had been too lost in the grip of the corruption of my sexuality, and by the time I realised it was stalking me and I turned to fight it, it was too late.

In the news at the time, men who had been exposed

as sexual predators kept using sex addiction as an excuse for what they had done, muttering words of trite contrition before sloping off for a week or two at an expensive rehab centre and hoping it might salvage their careers. It infuriated me. Sexual compulsion wasn't what made those men abusers, but toxic masculinity in cruel alliance with the abuse of positions of power. Callow columnists and pundits who looked as if they were barely capable of getting addicted to tea cited these losers to pooh-pooh the idea that sex might even be addictive. They said that those who claimed to suffer were greedy, just couldn't control themselves. Well, what is a loss of control if not a form of addiction? I've met enough predators to know that they are addicted to nothing except their power over someone weaker. I've also heard from others, in drunken confessions in quiet corners of pubs or in breaking sobs in the twilit intimacy of a post-fuck bedroom, anxious revelations of a problematic attachment to a sexuality where extremity has replaced intimacy, be that via promiscuity, violence or pornography. Often those inclinations seemed to have been moulded in the pre-adult past by older, preying hands.

Compounding the trauma of any relationship's aftermath, the agony of seeing Alice had been to be confronted by the broken part of myself that had in part caused it to end.

That night at KAOS, though, was different. For the first time her presence didn't send me into convulsions. Whenever a break-up happens friends will always tell you that the passing of time is the only solution to the agony, a piece of advice that is always far easier to give than receive, in part because it is the only truth of loss. I was sure that the intervening months had helped, but so had that moment in the Grunewald where I had turned from the beautiful man and those ugly old goblins who lurched along behind him. They had all melted away through the trees, for now at least. I danced my way past loss and jealousy, feeling the possibility of new paths opening up before me, before us. Outside the club we saw the sunrise together and there'd been no awkwardness, no anxiety. Before she'd taken a taxi home to E17 and I'd jumped on a bus to E5, we talked about going for a walk the next day.

The sun was hotter than it should have been for September when it blinded me at my front door at 7.19 a.m. It wasn't a day to be wasted. Knackered and hungover in the early afternoon, Alice and I WhatsApped for a while before arranging to meet on the train and walk from Chingford to Epping.

The end of love inevitably comes with pain, but when nothing too cruel has been done or said by either side its pangs can also be those of rebirth. The grassy plain was golden as a beach in the hot early autumn sun, and as we headed into the woods for once I didn't get us lost. It was the same route I'd walked that day months before when the apparition of the hanged man had sent me off into terror. There was no danger of that today.

We passed few people on our way as we caught up on work, family, friends and new relationships. The familiarity from the five years that we had spent together now bred ease, rather than sadness at its ending. This was the first time we'd been to the forest together as separate entities. I could feel the presence of High Beach Church away through the trees and not feel devastated that it was no longer a place shared.

We found the ramparts of Loughton Camp and climbed them from the north, taking photos in a hollow where a rune of sticks arranged in an arrow pointed towards a gap between the trees. I watched her walk their line, and the little familiar things she did, the turns of phrase, no longer hit me with the cruelty of nostalgia.

I spotted the skull of a fallow deer at rest under a gorse bush, a large flap of bristled rind unrotted but dry above the eye socket. She wrapped it in a cloth and put it in her bag to take home to clean and keep. A few years ago she'd found and picked the flesh from the skull of a Dartmoor pony with a forthright lack of squeamishness that touched so many aspects of her life. It was what I had fallen in love with. A while ago this would have set me off, but not today.

We stopped to drink water. The wind gusted a little, cooling us. I was wobbling with the heat and fatigue but the trees were solid, immovable, resisting the breeze with an immense power. My eyes saw the trunks emerging from the bracken and the mulch. But more than that, I felt myself dissolve into their unseen presence beneath, billions of roots and their mycelium of incalculable distance pushing through the soil, connecting, communicating, ensuring the survival of all this. At once I felt as if we were not a pair of souls drifting through the forest, but that it was endlessly changing and moving across us, a comb filtering away the wreckage and resentment left behind by what had once been so intimately close.

We left Epping Forest via a game of cricket on the pitch that sits above the M25 tunnel, and wandered through the town to the last stop on the Central Line. It wasn't dark, but as we rattled back through the fields the tainted windows of the carriage blackened the forest already embracing the night.

When she left with a quick hug to make the closing doors at South Woodford for an Uber back to what had once been our home I didn't feel the queasy ache that, for eighteen months, had marked our partings. I waited for my train under the bright towers of Stratford as tubes plunged down into the tunnel under London or rose to head out towards Debden, Loughton, Theydon Bois and Epping Forest. She texted me to say goodnight. The deer skull was already in a vat of bleach in her garden shed, becoming beautiful, something new.

20

The Valley of Light

The English autumn arrived a few weeks after that golden afternoon out on the edge of Berlin. Yet it was no less violent in its intensity and, for once, it took me with it. Across Epping Forest the beeches turned incandescent, the gnarled old pollards were no longer grotesque beasts but intricately carved candelabra holding up the season's fire.

I walked up to the forest twice that week trying to take it all in, the change of mood and the breaking of something. There was a clearing in my mind; a great hurricane had roared through and ripped away much of the dead and rotten matter. For years I had been walking through the same forest as the one in the picture on my parents' wall – thick, murky and twisted, blocking out the light of the sky. But now it looked as if a child had torn it from the frame and coloured it in with its brightest crayons.

I stood on a clay promontory that jutted into Strawberry Hill Pond. The water reflected the rippling, molten

229

colours of the trees and scored them deep into my eyes against the blue of the sky. All around was a gentle pattering as, like fizzing sparks, the leaves fell to the ground from the crucible of the canopy. In the psychedelic rain of fire I felt a dissolving of the senses, the uncovering of a memory as sight and smell and a rising euphoria became more powerful than the forgetfulness of time.

When I'd walked along the Pennine Way to Hebden Bridge in the earliest months of that spring I had skirted around the tops of Hardcastle Crags, a steep-sided valley that drains the moors. I'd wanted to conquer the summits, as well as myself, to connect with Stoodley Pike as a monument to an innocence and happiness that I naively believed might help guide my life.

I realised I'd been looking at the wrong part of the map. It was the woods of that deep valley that I ought to have gone to. I should have allowed the land to fall out beneath my feet as I walked from the emptiness of the moors, the moaning, rippling carpet of the heather, the sky that turns purple as it unleashes daggers of hail or rain that fills the bogs and floods pools, submerging even the stiles over the rough and broken dry-stone walls. I should have followed those rushing streams off the moor and down into the crags, because that's where I might have found the boy who I thought was lost and take his hand, to walk at once in my past and present.

My family would regularly make the drive down from Halifax through the grey ruins of the industrial Calder Valley to Hardcastle Crags. The light in Epping

Forest that afternoon took me back, three decades or more, to the times when I tottered hand in hand with Mum and Dad or sat on their backs in a contraption of steel tubes and canvas. I'd shake with their footsteps, my young eyes opened wide to the rippling lanterns of the autumn foliage and beech trees covered in moss so green that God might have borrowed my felt-tip pens to draw them. Mum's and Dad's voices would dance together in conversations that I was too young to understand. My ears had sung with their words of love just as they heard the stream rushing round the stepping stones and whispering to the wind in the treetops. All of them – Mum, Dad, nature – had the power of speaking in tongues.

On the edge of Strawberry Hill Pond, the falling Epping Forest leaves swirled with those in the Hardcastle Crags of my memory. The fingertips of the vision lingered for a while, then parted. I felt calm. A duck splashed down to land, and quacked.

The woods of Hardcastle Crags were as much a part of me as the memories from my Methodist childhood, which had fixed so many ideals and morals in my young mind. The autumnal vision, a kaleidoscope broken and swirling down the rocky valley, was no more or less alive in the deepest wells of myself than the musty books, click of the organ stops or laughter bouncing off the lino floor that was my experience of church. As a little boy I'd knelt on rough orange chairs in the church hall and looked out across the mill chimneys and roofs of the valley and up the wooded slopes to the moors beyond, and they were all there in me still, just like the hymns and the parables and smell of old Bibles and stewed tea. I could no more remove that than I could reach into the past and make myself run from those men. They were carvings of sorts that had been cut into me and would always be there, their meaning private to me.

A scar does not have to reopen into a wound, does not have to let in disease. It might be ignored if the rest of the growth is strong, if new life and new shoots are able to spring forth, be sustained, and the past not forgotten but managed somehow. That was what I had mistaken for so long. My adolescent years had me feeling such guilt and shame about my emerging sexuality that I had repressed so much. The pressure was too great to bear and I was pushed out into dangerous places where I encountered predators ready to snap me up. It hadn't helped that I was simultaneously assailed by the laddish masculinity of my peers. I rejected them, but they too ushered me into grasping arms.

There's an old tale I read as a child about a hedgehog being attacked by an adder. The hedgehog bites the end of the snake's tail and, rolling up into a ball, clamps down fast. The infuriated adder lashes out again and again at the hedgehog, trying to bite it, but in the end only sacrificing itself on its tormentor's spikes. It was a fine parable, with biblical resonance: the compulsive quest for ever more remote regions on the map of desire had ended up taking me to the point of self-destruction. Now, though, I understood that my fluid sexuality didn't need to be acted upon in order to exist. It was my own, to be judged by nobody aside from myself.

In Epping Forest the failure of the supposedly in-
fallible nature cure had forced me to confront myself
in a way that I had never done before. The forest had
become a place of hidden sexuality but one that I might
celebrate, even if its magic was no longer for me. In
that chest from the vestry of High Beach Church I'd
found the truth of an old family story and a cardinal sin
that had lanced the shaming eyes of God under which
I had struggled for so long. It wasn't God's forgiveness
that I sought, not least because I had finally started
to understand that nothing I had done had been a
'sin' in that damning, orthodox form. It was my own
pardon that I needed to accept, for all those times
when I had sinned against myself, letting others abuse
my body to debase the sacred and erotic possibility of
intimacy. That autumn I began to know it again, to
reclaim it, to know that intimacy can also mean 'into
me see'. Where once there had been thickets, now I
shone light.

Mia's text message had called me back from the Devil's Lake in Berlin, and over the following weeks I found
that those urges to destroy our future had become man-
ageable. We never found that swing in the forest again,
but with her acceptance of every element of who I was I
had an ally against the voices that muttered temptation
and judgement.

I no longer felt the quiver of compulsion in certain
parts of the forest. I had helped two lovers I know and
their friends, a lesbian couple who made DIY erotic
films, to find a location to shoot under the trees. As naked
bodies flickered through the surrounding underwood

a mewing came from above, and everyone looked up to see a buzzard circling over the clearing, a brown ghost of the daylight hours. I felt neither the sort of impetuous arousal that watching a sex film being made might previously have triggered, nor guilt in having enabled it. Instead, it was as if we'd documented the acting out of our most ancient connection with our woodlands.

The shooting of the film was the closing of a circle: Cosey Fanni Tutti's photographs in the forest in the 1970s had been, alongside the material in the archives, part of my growing understanding that there are no morals to nature, no right or wrong way to be or behave within it. It was Cosey rather than the child of Epping Forest, Genesis P-Orridge, who had illuminated it for me.

Cosey's voice had struggled to be heard, largely because Genesis had defined the artistic history of COUM and Throbbing Gristle. For all that Genesis was seen as a pioneer, it was Cosey's work that felt more honest, her engagement with Epping Forest more closely tied into the possibility it offered for an ancient spiritual connection rather than being a symbol of decadence. Through work I'd got to know Cosey fairly well and she became something of a mentor to me, almost an aunt figure who, with kindness and a wonderful no-bullshit attitude, always lived up to that mantra of hers. In it I saw an inner strength that I could understand and use for myself. It wasn't, I had begun to realise, all that dissimilar to the way in which my parents' faith shaped everything they did too.

Exoticised or intellectualised transgression is a convenient excuse for the failure of self-discipline. I saw that in myself. I saw it too in Genesis P-Orridge. A few years ago, Cosey published an account of her life in which she recounted the terrible abuse she'd suffered at Genesis' hands, years of coercion, control and physical violence. When Cosey finally ended the relationship and left, Genesis chased her down the street waving a massive knife. A few years later Genesis threw a block of concrete from a balcony that nearly hit Cosey's head. Had it done so it would have probably killed her.

Earlier in that perplexing year I had seen Genesis perform at the Serpentine Gallery, shuffling onto the stage to chant 'Humanity is a virus, humanity is a virus' in front of a psychedelic image that looked like a 1990s screensaver. The line was something of a cliché, used by anyone from the hackneyed comic Bill Hicks to the schlocky sci-fi flick *The Matrix*. It was preaching of a sort, but I'd seen my dad do far better from the pulpit at Methodist Central Hall just across St James's Park, with more power and feeling and love. When a few months later I tuned in to watch a live-streamed set by Genesis at the London arts venue Café Oto, it was the very same. 'Humanity is a virus, humanity is a virus.' It'd happened a third time too, at an event in Hull to celebrate the work of COUM Transmissions. Genesis stood onstage, intoning over and over, 'Humanity is a virus, humanity is a virus.' It was a shame to hear something that sounded so phoned in, even if for the devoted fans in the room it was a lesson from a guru.

It was a shame, too, because in the sound-check I'd seen earlier that day, Genesis had tested the mic by singing unaccompanied that funeral staple, the song that must have been played a thousand times in the East London Cemetery down at the south of the forest as the coffins slid behind the curtain to return human forms to dust: 'But more, much more than this / I did it my way.' I have rarely heard anything that sounded so hauntingly honest, so broken and alone.

Of those children of the forest who had shown me such different paths, one had turned out to be a false prophet.

As I've got older I've noticed how much more like my dad I've become. I've filled out the brown-leather jacket he bought in the 1960s with his first pay packet, working pitching hay on an Essex farm. I was always proud to be like him. I have long counted myself fortunate to have had such an example of love and grace that I could construct my own version of masculinity, even if the prejudices of some practitioners of the religion to which Dad had devoted his life had made it an anguished process. As we age, and our parents age, we approach a place of equilibrium; though we can never be equal as adults, an invisible umbilical cord will for ever remain uncut.

I felt this balance as I pushed Dad in a wheelchair through the outpatients' ward of the south London hospital where he'd been treated for prostate cancer. I felt his weight, all his person, the history that we've shared, the life and love he has given me, in the smooth glide of the wheels across the polished floor.

I had never seen Dad so tired and his spark so flickering, even if he had, true to form, spent much of his stay in hospital trying to help the others on the ward who had no family or friends to visit them. With a stark awareness of his mortality, of the inevitability of the cycle of generations, that had never been quite so acute before, I found myself wanting to do anything for him.

We are tied by blood and the shared memories that sit quietly in our past, always there, frozen in time. Our tendency is to look into those far-off days in order to attempt to untangle the codes, to work out what of ourselves is inherited, what might have passed unconsciously down the generations. If I was able to silence the shaming voice of judgemental Christianity I knew that I could find, via Mum and Dad, much of what had made me who I am. It was their great gifts of love that, in the end, had helped me start to try to save myself. An atheist might argue that this is because they are just preternaturally good people, but I am not so sure. In the strength of Dad's words from a pulpit or in the love of Mum's prayers, the offering up of the very core of herself, there was, is and always will be a curious spark that comes from beyond the human.

As Dad continued to recover from his operation, he spent the convalescence going through old files of correspondence and household bills. One evening, a message arrived on the family WhatsApp group. It was an iPhone snap of a photograph that Dad had forgotten for decades. I pinched the screen to zoom in on this curious black and white shot of an old man in an overcoat, formal tie and collar, his crispy white hair combed in a side parting with a single wave, sideburns and moustache flowing neatly down to a pointed beard. The eyes are deep-set atop a decidedly familiar nose in a slim face that has an almost quizzical expression. Underneath, in neat handwriting: 'With best love from Father, September 1926.' I swiped to the next image. It was of the back of the photo where, in Dad's handwriting, was written:

Uncle Bill told us at Aunt Eve's funeral that my great-grandfather was the result of a 'liaison' between one of the Baring family (bankers) and one of the maids. Mother a Turner? This photo is of the son, who became steward of Arabin House, High Beach, Epping Forest.

Thomas Charles Baring was the landowner who had paid for the building of the second High Beach Church where I had found so many of my ancestors buried. Unlike theirs, his grave is marked – a marble crucifix tops a large vault round the back of the building. A devout character, Dad's Uncle Bill wasn't the sort to have made up something like that. He must have heard the story from the horse's mouth, as it were, for Eve was George Turner's granddaughter and their lives overlapped for many years. I immediately went online to look at census records, but it's hard to place any of the Baring family in the High Beach area at the time. Perhaps Mary Ann had met Thomas Baring elsewhere. Maybe the story had become confused, and the father of her child was one of the other well-to-do men from the big houses of the forest. I suppose the exact details don't really matter. Whatever the liaison, and whoever it was with, I can only hope it was caused by love across the class divide. It seems more likely that it was coercion.

That night, Mary Ann Turner hovered indistinct in my slumbering mind. Who was this young woman who had had her son baptised at High Beach Church in the late summer of 1854?

The next day I downloaded my great-great grand-father George Turner's birth certificate from the website of the National Archives. His birth is listed as 24 June 1854, registered on 31 July. Just as in the baptism record, there's a blank where the father's name would ordinarily be. Mary Ann is listed as resident at Temple Row, East Ham. Further Googling and an email to my friend at the London Metropolitan Archives revealed that in later years it was often listed as Temple Row, Wakefield Street, and an old map of the area shows a small line of cottages in the middle of fields, next to which is marked a temple, perhaps a spiritual place or maybe an ornamental building for one of the large houses nearby.

I searched again and found Mary Ann on the 1851 census, a child aged fifteen living with her family a few fields away to the north, just to the south of Wanstead Flats on what would later become Epping Forest land.

The house, home to eleven people, was on Irish Row which, given the prejudices of the time, was probably an indicator of poverty. There's a building described as an 'animal charcoal works' just out the back. It was in those strange years when rural, remote Essex was starting to disappear underneath London, when factories and short rows of houses appeared among fields sliced through by the new railways, and the boundaries between city and countryside became increasingly blurred.

I wondered what had happened to Mary Ann over the next few years, how she came to take a bastard son the many miles to the tiny chapel of St Paul at High Beach. Perhaps that was the only place she could find where the child of an unmarried mother would be baptised. That seems unlikely, given the distance and the small size of the place of worship.

Whatever the situation, it seems to have ended with loss. She carried her boy the length of Epping Forest and, in a way, she left him in it. George vanishes in the 1861 census. There's a Mary Ann Turner working as a servant halfway between East Ham and High Beach in Woodford, but she doesn't appear to be with her son. After that, at some point in her twenties, she simply disappears.

I couldn't know, either, what Mary Ann Turner looked like as she clasped her baby to herself and travelled up through the forest to High Beach for that baptism. She'd have taken a very similar route to the one we took with my granny's body over a century later, but done it in reverse through what was then open woodland pasture or agricultural fields. The 'fallen woman' was a recurring character in the Victorian imagination, reflecting insecurities over the sexual agency of women, the myth of innocence threatened by the power of the city, and religious piety that cast shame and punishment before it did love. Our imaginations are always led by the art and literature of what has gone before, and for a while that is how I saw her, as one of those characters from a painting by Cruikshank or G. F. Watts. I glimpsed her cowed and huddled over the tiny form, trudging up a rutted lane through a landscape groaning with the thick growth of summer, eyed by the workmen who would have then been starting to enclose the forest land, the pollards looming over her as she walked with her baby, desperate to have his life and his birth sanctified by God.

I looked at the maps of the old roads and the new, at the photograph of the little boy as an old man, and I closed my eyes and tried to picture her walking through that place I loved and had loathed, so very different now from how it was then. I shrank the trees, demolished the houses, scraped the tarmac from the roads, replaced cars with carts and horses and there she was. But when she looked up, I saw that it was not Mary Ann at all but my mum. And she was holding me.

On 7 December 1978 Dad returned home from a meeting to find the carpet covered in blood and a note in an unfamiliar hand telling him to rush to hospital. There, he was told that his pregnant wife, still nearly two months off full term, had suffered a serious haemorrhage and that both she and his newborn son would likely die. They operated, and the news came that the boy was lost but his wife would survive. Later, the prognosis changed and it was thought the boy could in fact be saved, but would likely be seriously brain-damaged from the extended period without oxygen. My mum came round in the hospital ward and, half delirious, started yelling to anyone who would listen that she wanted to breast-feed. Those crucial moments of intimacy between mother and child, so necessary for a secure bond to be formed, were delayed by days.

Seconds after they emerge into the world newborn babies are assigned an Apgar Score on a scale of health that goes from zero (almost dead) to ten (presumably the nation's future rugger-buggers). It took me a while to get beyond one. While everyone was fighting to keep me alive, I was also missing out on those early moments which, though they fade from memory, psychologists believe score our psyche profoundly. Separated from Mum for many vital hours, I was confined to a plastic box, being fed through tubes instead of at her breast.

In picturing Mary Ann Turner on that lonely forest walk I saw the anxieties that always exist between a parent and a child. Those hours of separation at my own birth are beyond my conscious memory, but came to shape me nonetheless. That, and a guilt that I had nearly killed my own mother later became conflicted with religion, making it hard to believe that the love between a parent and a child might be stronger than that between an individual and the laws of God. I had thought that my inability to get angry with Mum or Dad for bringing me up with such destructive religious views was a failing on my part. It wasn't. I count myself fortunate not to have been raised in one of those families where blind adherence to whichever faith they might believe in is the victor.

Mum and Dad, the way I saw it, only inadvertently passed on the harsh judgements on sexuality that came with the word of God, my third parent. I had been wrong to develop this panic that they could not accept me the way I was. Their faith was made of compassion, love and understanding, not wrath and judgement. *That* had developed within my own weirdly fundamentalist interpretation of scripture, or the bigoted whispers I heard outside my immediate family that had, like a rot or canker, eaten away at me for so long.

On my laptop I opened a folder of thousands of images I'd saved over the past year. Almost outnumbering the photographs of the pollards in all their odd beauty were the snapshots I'd taken of keepers' reports, legal documents, newspaper articles on conservation, scandal and murder. Queen Victoria had only been half right when she proclaimed Epping to be 'the people's forest' in pomp and ceremony at a huge event up at King's Oak in 1882. The forest itself had proved to have remarkable agency of its own, possessing those who crossed its threshold. So many of the stories I had found were of people who entered the forest and remained for ever changed by the experience.

In my family, the forest came and went across the

generations, three of which were buried within it. Mary Ann Turner took her child into it in search of God's blessing. From it Mum and Dad had derived their joy in Creation. I had entered it in search of a key that might free me from the cage of shame. It seemed to loom there, always, even in the simplest of ways.

I flicked through a forgotten folder of photos I'd taken of that box of postcards that had revealed the secret of my family's past. There was one I'd not really noticed at the time, sent from Eve, my dad's aunty and the source of that photograph, to her father Ted, early in the twentieth century. The picture on the front was of High Beach Church and on the back she'd written:

Dear Dad, I thought this might interest you. Heard a fine talk about High Beach on Wireless on Tuesday. Had a nice day at the show, hope you are well.

It hadn't meant much to me when I'd first seen it – it was merely a means by which to place the family in the forest at the right time to try and explain my mystery. High Beach Church looked different on the postcard, the trees that surrounded it being far lower than they are now, a century later. For all the mystery of George Turner's birth and its place in my own drama, for a while the story of the Turners in Epping Forest was that of just another family trying to get on with their lives.

It was the same for all the forest families, for we are all forest families. Like the Willingales and all those other lives now only still breathing in unseen papers in forest files, the trees came and went within our story. The forest and the human danced around one another. It made me think of the Victorian newspapers with their illustrations of the November lopping ceremonies up on Staples Hill, the flickering light and figures casting long shadows against pollards that writhed overhead as if they were participants in the ritual – which of course they were. Obsessed as ever by the pictures, I determined to go up to Staples Hill to mark the moment, as close to the date as I could. I waited until a morning close to the anniversary when my weather app promised a frosty start.

I walked against a tide of commuters carrying cups of coffee that steamed like censers, past Lopping Hall and its over-door carving of a man with billhook raised, and up through the street of cottages that once were the slums where the Willingale family lived. The light of the rising sun silhouetted the school building on Staples Road and the door marked 'Boys' where Dad and Neil Megson had tottered all those decades ago, and I crossed the clearing crisped with the first frost of the year to head up the sharp slope to the top of the hill. In the century and a bit since that final ceremonial lopping the neglected pollards had sent up huge new poles towards the sky, five, six or seven thick limbs coming from the old trunks. It was a moment that had been fixed in time, but one that had given each tree, and the forest as a whole, a new future.

These giants let barely any light reach the ground. Beneath their canopy, nothing much grows. Across the brown leafy wasteland the morning sun silhouetted the shapes of those thick trunks and the soaring limbs, and their shadows stretched towards me. Perhaps they reached out to quietly wonder where the people had gone, those who once worked them, who made them what they were.

21

Sap Lust

That autumn was the finest I'd ever known in the forest, made more beautiful by its sudden ending with the first hard frost and strong blow of the season. It was mostly only the oaks, always the last to shed and sprout, that still held on to a threadbare scatter of brown as the treetops flickered under the fireworks of November.

Mia was with me as we sploshed across the plain, now starting to return to its boggy winter state. We'd found a new way to communicate whereby I no longer created barriers to the place where we might meet in understanding. In the distance a chainsaw whined through the autumn air. It got louder, the farting buzz of the blade on wood drowning out our conversation as we turned the corner of the ride. The frantic mechanical racket suddenly dropped to a satisfied mutter, replaced by cracking timber and the rush of falling branches, like an old broom across a stone floor. There were trunks of birch and beech piled in pyramids ten or so high. A sign of a falling man warned children to stay away.

Sawdust twinkled in eddies across the scene of destruction, settling on mud smeared across the forest floor by tractor tyres. Holly lay shredded as if a wolf had been at a Christmas door. Away from the ride, as the land rose towards High Beach, the cleared forest floor was pockmarked by the light brown of freshly made stumps. It was beautiful.

Epping Forest is at its most dense in the area north of Chingford Plain. I found the leap from the light, open spaces of the grassland into the thickets disturbing, and it would set my mind awry. The more I had come to understand the forest, the more I felt saddened by how dishevelled and choked it had become. The claustrophobic gloom was eerily inert, with barely a squirrel to tip the countless branches. Once I heard a woodpecker hammering at the dead white bone of an oak and it sounded like the croaking of an infernal toad. What would have been individual pollards standing in woodland pasture were now clawed at by halos of holly that closed out the light and drowned the forest floor. Where once there had been glades, now thickets of beech saplings were the iron bars of a gaol. Many had died losing their quest for light yet remained upright. I would crash my way through, pushing the trees aside like Samson between the temple pillars.

The area Mia and I stumbled across had once been like that. Today it was being utterly transformed by the chainsaw-wielding conservationists who scuttled across it like efficient beavers. The ribbon of cleared ground curved to the north and the open grassland of Whitehouse

Plain. Old pollards stood in the pools of light across the clearing, looking triumphant in the space that had been denied them for decades. Some young beech had been left but had been pollarded and now stood across the open land, bare poles that held the promise of centuries more life.

One of the arborists, draped in climbing rope and safety gear like some sort of specialist commando, came over to say hello. The conservationists' work, he explained, was part of the Epping Forest Management Plan to try and restore some of the woodland pasture that had been consumed by the rewilding of Epping Forest. The plan didn't cover the whole of the forest – some parts were being left to carry on as they pleased – but there was a strategy to control the slow invasion of choking birch and holly that had happened after the ending of lopping and, later, grazing. This, he explained, would help to see the return of threatened flora and fauna typical to the old woodland pasture and lowland heath landscape – orchids, heather, lizards and other reptiles. There was also a long-term goal to see the return of the nightingale, once common on the plains but now vanished along with its habitat, to Epping Forest. The arborist asked if I'd like to get involved. I told him I was sure my terrible co-ordination meant that I shouldn't be trusted with a chainsaw. He laughed, and told me to have a look online for one of the conservation groups open to the public to join. I thanked him and we headed off.

Excited, I told Mia about my favourite human story of the forest, one I had uncovered right at the start of my plunge into the archives in that depressed quest for distraction a year before.

Early in the morning of 13 August 1942, Ordinary Seaman Edward Charles Lankester was floundering, half drowned yet seared by the Mediterranean sun, in the sea a few miles off the coast of Tunisia. His ship, HMS *Manchester*, had been sunk by Italian torpedoes just after 1 a.m. Lankester wasn't a confident swimmer. A shipmate later recalled that before long he was barely moving, his cork life vest just keeping his face above the surface. Lankester begged his friend not to leave him alone.

Lankester was born on 5 December 1909 and christened five days later with a splash of holy water from the font of High Beach Church. He became a woodsman, working day and night to lop and fell, clear the underwood, absorbing forest lore with every falling of the leaves. By the early years of the Second World War he was an acting keeper, but before long was conscripted into the Royal Navy. During his training he sent the first in a series of carefully written letters to Superintendent McKenzie, his forest boss. These were what I'd found in the blue files of the London Metropolitan Archives. Lankester's letters had jumped out at me more than any poem or story composed about the forest, more than any of the worthy letters and diatribes written about how it ought to be saved or cared for.

He wrote about how he'd rather not be posted to a battleship (there's 'too much spit & polish'), before the tone of his words suddenly changed from matter-of-fact, dutiful almost, to wistful: 'I expect the trees in the forest will soon be changing colour. I am looking forward to the time when I can again work in the forest, which I miss very much, but that seems to be a long way off . . . This seems to be the first year that I have not heard the cuckoo, or seen a swallow, that I can remember.'

On 12 June 1942 he sent a final letter from HMS *Manchester*. 'I bet the forest is looking grand, and I would love to have a stroll through it at the moment, as I have not seen a tree for weeks, and it is surprising how you miss them. Please remember me to the gang sir and tell them I am looking forward to the time when I shall be back with them.'

Two months and one day later HMS *Manchester* was at the bottom of the sea. Lankester's intense yearning for the forest had struck me because he, like the man who lived in the forest, had a love for it that was heightened by his abrupt departure for the unforgiving metal of a warship and the prospect of sudden death. Behind the deference to his boss spoke a voice that didn't suggest some stout and macho man of the woods but a sensitivity with which I could identify.

I might not have been able to do what the man who dwells in the forest suggested, and join him for a life of manuka honey, rain showers and starlit nudism on the golf course. Nor was I able to feel entirely free in the furtive corners of the bushes around Eagle Pond. But after that conversation with the arborist, I felt I might be able to follow the Willingales, Lankester and those of my own family who were listed as agricultural labourers and gardeners on the edge of the forest for nearly 200 years and engage with the place, a blade in my hand.

Although I had a weapon, it wasn't to be a fight. This wasn't like those times when I had wandered through the forest and felt as if I were in a battle with 6,000 acres of trees, when I couldn't stop myself taking that train to Chingford to be defeated by them, over and over again. That was a battle I couldn't win.

As soon as I got home I Googled 'voluntary work Epping Forest' and came across the website of the Epping Forest Conservation Volunteers. There were photographs of people with saws and loppers, bonfires, stumps. It looked like it might be a hoot. I scanned a list of forthcoming tasks in the forest, inviting volunteers to join most Tuesdays and Sundays for a 9.30 a.m. start from the Forest HQ at the Warren. Bring stout boots. All welcome.

My teenage dread of PE and the testosterone-fuelled threat of a gathering of men had always made me wary of big groups, but I needn't have worried about the EFCV. At first I hovered quietly at the edge of the group, but the twenty-ish souls who make it up to the forest every weekend turned out to be a welcoming bunch. Friendly talk was of the fortunes of West Ham, bird feeders, Netflix box sets. There were tree experts, prog-rock fans, beekeepers and hedge layers. As I sat eating a lunch-break sandwich on that first autumn session I noticed a quiet love of the forest and of nature, not expressed gushily but in shared fragments of information, questions carefully answered.

I went up as often as I could for the rest of that year, gradually feeling my way into the work and a different kind of connection with the forest. Safety rules and the risk of accidentally dropping a tree on another volunteer's head meant that our work was usually fairly solitary, though I was always conscious of being part of the group, within the area defined by tape and marked by boards warning the public of falling trees. I liked it like this. It reminded me of church, being a largely silent individual at the heart of a collective experience devoted to a higher purpose.

You might call it sap lust, I suppose, the energy that takes hold when a saw is in your hand and all around young trees climb towards the sky. The urge to cut and lop and fell is primal. The saw slices straight through the topography of the tree bark, like a road across the contours of a map. With every stroke the tree rattles and murmurs as if in resignation or regret. Dead wood is dislodged and comes crashing down.

For bigger trees, we use a gob cut: saw down through the trunk at a thirty-degree angle, and then make another horizontal cut to meet it about a quarter to a third of the way through the trunk. Knock the wedge out, then saw across, slightly higher up from the removed gob, and the tree will creak, lean, crack and then whoosh down in the direction you've sent it.

After a few trunks have been felled, you start noticing how different trees react. Hazels seem to go pretty easily, consistently resistant all the way through. On a silver birch the bark and outer rings crackle away under the teeth of the saw, as do the scrub oaks. But these seem to emulate their bigger cousins, and the centre of the trunk is frequently an absolute bugger to get through. Still, it seems that being a volunteer woodsman is one of the few jobs where blaming your tools is actively encouraged, and nobody really minds if you go in search of a saw with a sharper blade.

The sharper the blade, the higher the note of the crackle through the bark and the wood. Sawdust, tiny particles of the tree's history, falls around my feet. I sweat. The tree falls. Another.

We are used to encountering trees at trunk level, where their power and strength seems so profound (it always stuck in my head that if you are unlucky enough to drive a car into a tree at speed you are essentially crushing it and yourself against the entire mass of the earth) as to be unassailable. People hug the trunks of trees because they speak of life and offer a connectivity to nature. We've developed a morality when it comes to nature that says that to interfere with it is sacrilegious. It's a judgement as perverse as that of branding queerness a sin.

When we imagine the forest, it is the trunks that we picture, powering up from the ground. Taken down from their altitude the leaves become a marvel, as does the unique patina of the tiniest twigs that until just seconds ago had been beckoning to the clouds. There's such delicacy in the tiny eddies between leaf and clouds, sun and rain, that tiny twigs might perhaps feel indivisible from the sky. They're nothing compared to even the spindliest trunk of a sapling yet must follow it down, the tip of every twig drawing a chaotic geometry, trailing a shower of dead leaves as it falls.

It's strange to see the trees of Epping Forest like this,

up close, the great piles of cut beech and hornbeam, birch and holly saplings on their sides all topsy-turvy. Sometimes when I have felled a tree, I walk the length of its trunk and round the crown, taking in the view that only birds and insects have seen before. It is never a moment of exultation – I do not find myself standing over the tree as a hunter might pose for a picture over the body of his recently shot quarry. Instead I feel as if I am floating around this creature, really seeing it for the first time.

Each stump is a bright new island cut into the forest floor. I'd blow off the dust and count the rings, ten, twenty or thirty years of time that I'd use to transport me back into my own life. At first each ring might give a jolt as it reminded me of a mistake or regret, but as the months went on I realised that I could see them representing change, acceptance, learning my way to a future.

One Sunday a small boy stood watching us, turned to his mum and said, 'Why are those people cutting down the trees that help us breathe?' He needn't have worried. There'd be plenty left. The felling of some of the trees here, where we're working to preserve the old wood-land pasture, does not create an absence. The greater organism, the forest, still remains. I began to realise that this was as much about affirming our human rela-tionship with the woods as it was about conservation of a landscape. Each session with the volunteers is a tiny nibble at eternity, fruitless in its own way, for most cut stumps more than a year or so old have a halo of new growth. The roots of the tree are always still there under the ground, unconsciously plotting. The holly and the hazel might once again tower over the grasses and wild flowers that my felling has helped return to this landscape, and in turn drown them in a pool of shade.

For days after a session in the forest the pains in my body attest to the feeling of being part of nature. My arms and legs, muscles strained by unfamiliar tasks, are crotchety and stiff, as if the sedentary lifestyle of desk and tube and pub and bus and bed has given them a taste of something they crave. There are scratches, welts and bruises to remind me. Getting into the shower or bath is to be covered with electric shocks of pain. The area round a wasp sting remains red for days afterwards, and when I brush my lips against the spot the skin still feels oddly warm.

During those days working in the forest I felt closer to myself than I ever had back in London, the gibbering voices of anxiety, doubt and awkwardness silenced by the rasping of the saw. Nothing had ever made me feel like this before, an overwhelming surge of contentment. In those moments I know who I am. In every wince of pain coursing through my body I can feel it, the skin touching the summer heat or winter chill of the forest air. I have always felt that going to the gym is a futile way to exercise, a challenge only against the self, or the egos of competitors, the kind of exercise that other people do; my experiences at school and body-loathing have rendered it impossible for me. A towel discarded en route to the shower can also turn the changing room into a place that can trigger self-destructive behaviour. But this was entirely different. Every time I went there to work and bring new aches and pains back with me to the city, I felt the sourness in my relationship with the forest start to fade. The fatigue is different to the exhaustion I have felt after plunging into the damp, hateful recesses of compulsion. It's as if I have given my energy, my thought and my sweat to the forest. It is the most ancient exchange of which I have ever been a part.

The reconciliation between my past and present selves stayed with me a little longer each time I made the trip. I was banishing my awkwardness, reclaiming my body and enjoying it not for how it looks or what might be done to it by others, but for how it works.

The forecast had promised heavy rain on that particular Sunday, in the no-man's-land of January when the year does not quite believe it has arrived. I took the early train to Chingford, sharing a carriage with a young couple on their way home from some club, collapsed against one another, chins twitching with the exertion of the post-E gurn. Leaving the station, I crossed into the forest and walked the high ground by Queen Elizabeth's Hunting Lodge towards the rendezvous at the Warren. Out over the treetops the spire of High Beach Church was hidden in the morning mist, and only a few magpies flapped from tree to tree. I kept stopping to send photos to Mia and my phone buzzed with her replies, intimate despatches from her bed back down the line. The glow of her naked warmth dispelled the chill gloom of the winter forest and rose within me. When we were overwhelmed together, neither God nor the grasping ghosts stood round our bed, judging or cajoling. Here was love as love should be.

We'd been set a tough task to do, out on Jericho Plain where silver birch had, in just a few decades, filled up what was once open heathland. The air was cold and damp, exertion dragging it into lungs, soaking out coughs. A good crowd had turned up, but everyone lingered round the pile of brash as the fire took hold within it, waiting for the small flames carefully set on a pile of twigs to catch and start to crackle up through the frozen air. An infant fire needs coaxing, but once it really starts going it devours the cut wood, even the thickest logs, ravenously, the tongue of flame licking at the sky.

More and more wood went on the fire, the pile shrinking. People stood with their backs to the conflagration or held out soaked gloves to steam them dry. The group leader spotted me staring into the blaze. He gave a terrific, cracking laugh. 'Look at you! Staring at where we're all going to end up!'

Who knows what the natural aspect of Epping Forest will be in a hundred years when I am dead and forgotten. Those small square metres that were once Jericho Plain where I'd sweated and laboured might once more be choked by scrub, or perhaps they'll end up as open forest floor underneath tall beech crowns. The effort of those few Sunday hours will have changed the forest for a while just as it changed me. In my rediscovery of my body was a lightness, and hope of new beginnings. It might be temporary, for the mind is never entirely set free from the entanglements it grows for itself. Now, though, I had the tools with which to cut them back, a fire with which to burn.

The smoke rose in thick swirls against the trees, which in winter are far more varied in their browns, duns and seaweed hues than the flat and choking green of midsummer. Above the treetops, though, it became indistinct against a thick grey sky that promised a change in the weather.

22

Out of the Woods

The next day snow falls as it often does in the city, alive only for those few seconds of white static against red buses, dirty roofs, bricks and windows closed against a gloomy morning. Into the thick, dull grass outside the flats, against the pavement and on the warm tops of cars, the perfect yet invisible geometry of the flakes is annihilated in an instant, for ever unseen.

I have seven minutes until the train departs from Hackney Downs. A half-formed notion sends me into the booth under the bridge outside the station to spend a fiver on two bunches of daffodils, their flowers already open. I stuff them into the side pocket of my rucksack. Creaking from the previous day's exertions, I slowly pull myself up the stairs to the station platform.

I had wanted to see how the man who lived in the forest was faring in this cold snap, the first one since he'd told me about his plans for an olive-oil thermometer so many months before. I'd called my aunty, but she told me that he was no longer in his camp. When I'd spoken to him he'd been so adamant that he'd not be leaving until he himself became a forest spirit that I worried that the golfers had organised to remove him against his will. I couldn't bear to think of him imprisoned, away from his place of salvation. But no, my aunty said, he was happy enough to be in the sheltered accommodation that had been provided for him. He just needed new knees. The forest remains in him though, I am sure of that, and he in it. But I'm not going to see him on this cold January day. Today I am visiting the dead.

This thin railway line, sharply curving up after Wood Street towards Chingford, had been a chute for me the past couple of years. I'd often not wanted to go to the forest, unable to trust the way that my mind would react to being there. Where the buffers are at Chingford Station it had once been intended that an embankment would carry the tracks through the forest to take trippers to High Beach. The line was never built, but I've sometimes felt, when the train stops, that a momentum was propelling me forwards in a way that I did not quite understand. On many wanders up there I wished I hadn't gone, but I feel quite different now. I get off the train and with the sparkling chill of the snowflakes on my cheeks I feel so alive. I smile, for those of us prone to depression have to make the best of a break in the weather.

No snow has settled on the plain though it is still falling, the distant trees floating in and out of view through the swirling grey. A cyclist labours towards me across the rough ground, his fluorescent yellow jacket the only brightness in the woolly mass ahead.

From under my boots comes the familiar squelch of the waterlogged winter plain. I walk through puddles that clean off the mud from a walk in the Calder Valley a fortnight ago. I like the thought that muck from the Yorkshire valleys of my birth is mingling with the ancient loam of Essex from where my family had come.

Thanks to my friend at the archive, I've discovered that in the 1891 census George Turner's profession is listed as the sexton of High Beach Church. That was the very year Charles Baring died and was interred in his family vault at the back of the church. Had that story written on the back of the photograph of George been true, he would likely have had to bury his own father without being able to acknowledge him as such.

Last night, as I travelled back from Jericho Plain it had occurred to me that I ought to find the site of the first High Beach Church where George Turner had been baptised, to walk to the new churchyard where he lay and conduct a ritual that might unite them all, the rumours and truths and fictions, the contradictions and many griefs of my family and all the families of the forests, of all the forests.

The snowfall is no more picturesque here than it was back in London, just cold and sharp and refusing to settle, and I have the Green Ride to myself.

The original St Paul's High Beach was a simple building, written about by John Clare as tucked away and half smothered by the forest:

So beautiful the Chapel peeps between
The hornbeams with its simple bell; alone
I wander here, hid in a palace green.

According to the modern OS map and forest books nothing of it now remains. Earlier I'd screen-grabbed images from Victorian maps that marked it as a little black dot in its own rectangular forest clearing. As I walk up Church Road past the asylum where Clare once lived, hands shivering on the glass of my phone, I swipe between the worn sepia of the antique maps and the blue dot on Google's satellite photograph until the curve in the way and an old hedge alignment seem to point towards the right spot. I turn to the right, off the road, and look into the snow-flecked forest. There, clear as anything, is a rectangular C-shape in the forest floor, three trenches of murky water where walls must once have stood.

When I found the baptism of my great-great-grandfather in the dusty vestry all those months ago it was as if I heard his voice whispering across the centuries. I hear it again now. The hairs on the back of my neck tingle with more than just the cold as I pass through where the church door must have been. It's so strange to be in a place that is no longer there but still houses everything I have been looking for all this time. The wet ground has given up fragments of the old building, and as I process around the carpet of leaves I find roof tiles, a piece of rusted ironwork. Shining through the autumn leaf fall is a lump of stone, whitewashed as pure as the falling snow. I pick it up and carry it to where the altar would have been on the far side. Now there is just the hollow stump of a young and broken tree. I will make a new altar, with the stone.

The centre of the dead trunk doesn't seem to have a bottom and I fleetingly picture it as a magical mirror back to the nineteenth century. I feel the presence of Mary Ann Turner beside me as she hands over her little boy to be baptised. In the name of the Father, the Son and the Holy Ghost. I am back in the forest on the night when I was at my lowest ebb and my nephew was born on the other side of the world. I am back in the moment of my own birth.

I place the whitewashed stone next to the trunk. I unwrap the daffodils and rest them on it, leaning the stems against the stump. Compared to the dank rot of the mulch and the cold, dead air of the winter forest the smell of the flowers is as rich and sickly as incense. I breathe deeply of the heady smell and the cold of the forest.

I step back, take off my hat and say a prayer to the God who has shaped me, to the forest, to my family and to love. The forest is silent aside from the drops of melted snow from the trees. My head is full of hymns.

A blizzard of individual histories whirl through our cities and our forests. Immersed within them, we have to let our minds be carried on their currents and rise or fall like the lightest leaf. We are never out of the woods because the woods are part of us, our terrors and pleasures, our sorrow, our joy, our grief and our desires. Underneath their cover we can be whosoever we want, for there are no rules or contradictions here. We can live our finest life, or our worst. We can even end it. Just as we can never leave our families, neither their DNA nor the hold of their love, the forest is part of all of us. In that acceptance is rage and sensuality, terror and ecstasy, blind confusion, ignorance and curiosity. They are just as much a part of us as we are of them. The forests strip us naked and tease us, they fuck us raw. Yet they also hold our stories, mute, tender as a newborn in a mother's arms, its ears deaf and uncomprehending to her murmurs of love.

I feel the shape of the cold, empty square around me as if for a second the walls of High Beach Church have become solid again, out of the air. I feel the calm that I had known when Ian reappeared in the house that silenced the city, or in Mum's tender songs of God. In the trees beyond I see the picture that had so obsessed me on my parents' wall. That hunched and bedraggled figure isn't disappearing into the woods any more. He wasn't drawn with a romantic notion of the sublime. This was no Arcadia. Yet he wasn't, as I had thought when I drove along the road that broken day a year ago, about to be swallowed by the forest. Now I saw him entering the woods to embrace the chaos, preparing to be transformed.

At my stone altar I take away three-quarters of the daffodil stems and walk backwards out of the spectre of the church. I nod back towards the drop of colour, then turn and climb the oozing slope towards the second High Beach Church that was built by the man who may have been my three-times-great-grandfather, my boots slip-scoring through the muck.

In the summer the stones of the church crash from the surrounding foliage like a rocky outcrop from a receding wave, but now in the winter they merge into the cold branches in a crazed mesh. It is almost as much of an apparition as its own vanished forebear. I open the gate and walk into the churchyard. I pull out my phone again, to look at a picture I've saved of the old plan of graves that tells me where the body of my great-great-grandfather, both his wives and two of his three sons will be. They were poor and have no memorials, but the approximate spot can be found next to a thick oak stump. This is my second altar of the forest. I take another quarter of the flowers and place them down in cruciform. I step back and again say the prayer.

I walk around the church, to the Baring vault. It's gloomier and damper here, just a few feet separating the church wall from the ancient woodland. I place half of the remaining daffodils in the flower pot at the foot of the monument, step back and turn away from the church to face into the trees. It feels as it always has since as a child I first stepped into their mystery, that there could be nothing else and they must go on until the end of the world.

Standing by the low iron fence that separates the consecrated ground from the woods, I take the remaining daffodils and throw them, the bright petals arcing out into the trees beyond, catching what little light there is under the winter canopy in vivid pools of yellow. They are for Mary Ann, whose ghost has revealed the truth of this forest that sits silent and cold and loaded with the expectation of spring.

I am fixed there for a while. The snow stops falling. A motorbike growls in the distance and a blackbird behind me in the churchyard begins to chink chink chink in exasperation, wanting me gone.

I turn towards the road to walk to Ernie's tea hut for a brew, pulling out my phone to call Mum and Dad.

Acknowledgements

I have unfathomable depths of gratitude to those who have made this book possible. Most of all to my family for their understanding, kindness and permission to allow me to be as honest as I had to be. To Milène Larsson for her patience and tolerance and for giving me the key to reaching not just the heart of this book but also how to get to grips with love. To the endless good humour and encouragement of my agent Natalie Galustian, without whom I'd have given up on this years ago. To my editor Jenny Lord for spotting my story lurking in the trees long before I had seen it myself and guiding me to how it should best be told. To Jeff Barrett, Diva Harris, Robin Turner, Andrew Walsh and all at Caught by the River for their never-ending enthusiasm and support in publishing the 'Notes From Epping Forest' columns that were the seeds from which *Out of the Woods* grew. To Barry and Jane Turner, for years of teaching me to love the forest and most of all for bringing me to the man who lived in the woods. I owe a huge debt of knowledge to Claire Titley for guiding me through the musty boxes and faded records at the London Metropolitan Archives. A similar appreciation to Rob St John for introducing me to so much writing on the latest thinking around forests and nature, even if I did always get stuck on 'ontology'. Amy Liptrot, Ben Myers, Adelle Stripe, Rory Gibb, Tim Burrows, for knowledge and encouragement. Jen Allan, for mutual support and defying the library boredom. Also to Jen and Mark Williamson, Laura Cannell, Andre Bosman, Bethan Lloyd Worthington for collaborative adventures beyond the forest. Kirsteen McNish's support, including but not limited to inviting me to speak and read at her brilliantly curated events, has been a huge boost to my confidence.

Writing in London is a thankless task, so gratitude to Malcolm Anderson and Ros Mitchell for the use of Savages Cottage at the start of the writing process, and Mike Jay and Louise Burton for Little Woodfield, where I learned to not be afraid of the woods and the night. To Mark Pilkington, Lilith Whittles, Joe Whittles, Ellie Broughton, Laura Snoad and Andrew Walker for their kindness in welcoming me in when home felt like an impossibility. To the memory of Ian Johnstone for the same, and Daniel O'Sullivan and Alexander Tucker for opening the door to 147 Tower Gardens. For Cosey Fanni Tutti and Chris Carter for opening my eyes to new ways of living. To my Quietus colleagues past and present for allowing me the flexibility to get this written – John Doran, Anna Wood, Paddy Clarke, Christian Eede, Sophie Coletta, Laurie Tuffrey, Mat Colegate,

Bobby Barry and Karl Smith. This book was made possible by the generous support of a grant from the Society of Authors.

My thanks also to Amy Wevill, Holly Harley and Virginia Woolstencroft at W&N, Bill Drummond, Revd Hopkins at High Beach Church, Ruth Bayer, Lee Brackstone, Dan Papps, Alison Tappley, Suze Olbrich at Somesuch Stories, Ophelia Aasa, Craig Burston, Sue from the pub, Jeremy Deacon, David Moats, Glen Mcleod, Joanna Zawadzka, Robert Macfarlane, Bernie Brooks, Kristen Gallerneux, Tom Braham, Mat Schultz, Gosia Płysa and all at Unsound Festival, Jan Rolfe and all at CTM Festival, Amy Cutler, James Kirby, Richard Skelton, Harry Sword, William Doyle, Leo Chadburn, the Woodbine Inn, Zoe Miller, Eva Vermandel, Lynne Kaye and all at the Epping Forest Conservation Volunteers.

And of course to the man who lived in the forest, wherever he might now be.

There are organisations which can help those who have been affected by childhood sex abuse. CPPD London helped me to understand its impact in a way I never could have by myself. Organisations such as SurvivorsUK and One in Four offer invaluable resources to survivors. I'd urge anyone affected by this depressingly common issue to seek out their support and help in forever pushing those unwanted hands away.

Notes

p.13 Oliver Rackham, *Woodlands* (HarperCollins, London 2006) p.393

p.119 Ursula K. Le Guin, *The Wind's Twelve Quarters & The Compass Rose*, (Gollancz, London 2015) p.167

p.148 Stephen Humphries, *A Secret World Of Sex: Forbidden Fruit, The British Experience 1900–50* (Sidgwick & Jackson, London 1988) p.208

p.154 Derek Jarman, *Modern Nature: The Journals Of Derek Jarman* (Vintage, London 1992) p.85

p.173 Elliott O'Donnell, *Haunted Britain* (Consul Books, London 1948) p.142

p.180 Patrick Carnes, *Out of the Shadows: Understanding Sexual Addiction* (CompCare Publisher, Minneapolis 1983) p.181

p.196 Gaston Bachelard, *Poetics of Space* (Beacon Press, Boston 1958) p.197

South Dublin Libraries

www.southdublinlibraries.ie